DATE	ISSUED TO

© DEMCO 32-2125

V.A. DE LUCA is a member of the Department of English at the University of Toronto.

Thomas De Quincey: The Prose of Vision is the first full-length critical study of De Quincey's imaginative writings. Considering these writings as a 'prose of vision' transcending their origins in magazine journalism, the author stresses their relationship to the Romantic traditions of imaginative vision and inward quest. He traces continuing themes and their transformations throughout De Quincey's career, and he offers sustained critical readings of De Quincey's major works.

Professor De Luca discusses, in chronological sequence, the original version of *Confessions of an English Opium-Eater*, in which De Quincey traces his passage from innocence to experience; Gothic tales and essays on murder, which reveal a fascination with the concept of power; and the major works of De Quincey's later years, including *Suspiria de Profundis*, *The English Mail-Coach*, and the revised *Confessions*, which show the richest development of his interest in vision and in self-exploration. The book concludes with a discussion of the equivocal implications in De Quincey's three late major works and relates these implications to equivocal tendencies in the Romantic tradition itself – its uneasy yearning for transcendence and its courageous commitment to the flow of ordinary experience.

This study, which makes a significant contribution to an understanding of De Quincey's works, will be of particular interest to students of Romanticism.

V.A. DE LUCA

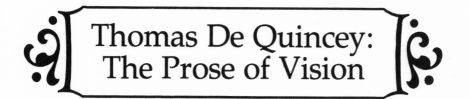

Thomas De Quincey:
The Prose of Vision

UNIVERSITY OF TORONTO PRESS
Toronto Buffalo London

© University of Toronto Press 1980
Toronto Buffalo London
Printed in Canada

ISBN 0-8020-5480-3

Canadian Cataloguing in Publication Data

De Luca, V.A., 1940-
Thomas De Quincey
Bibliography: p.
Includes index.
ISBN 0-8020-5480-3
1. De Quincey, Thomas, 1785-1859 – Criticism and
interpretation.
PR4537.D44   821'.8   C80-094412-7

TO MY MOTHER
AND THE MEMORY OF
MY FATHER

❧ Contents ❧

⚘] Preface [⚘

The writings of Thomas De Quincey that still live for us as imaginative literature form what may be called a prose of vision, a prose marked by pervasive transcendental concerns, by an aggrandized inwardness, and by conspicuous renderings of dreams and hallucinatory states. This prose displays clear affinities with much that is central in Romantic poetry, particularly the aspiration to capture and recreate the workings of the imagination and the experience of the sublime. The presence of such aspirations in De Quincey's work has ensured for it continued recognition from literary critics, and yet that recognition has been curiously vague. Often acknowledged as an artist, he is rarely described as a maker of artistic wholes; the intricate turns of his consciousness fascinate, but their relevance to what is permanent in our literary tradition remains ambiguous.

The aim of this study therefore is to offer a full critique of De Quincey's imaginative achievement, comprehending matters of form and meaning. Through commentaries on particular works, chronologically arranged, and through pursuit of thematic continuities I have sought to document his artistry and trace his imaginative development. The visionary program of the Romantics provides, finally, an implicit frame for my treatment. Seen in this context, De Quincey's literary career emerges as a kind of epic, fragmentary but powerful, an epic of the inner self in all its desolations and sublimities.

But in order to view De Quincey's career in this coherent way criticism must overcome the formidable obstacles posed by certain peculiar and unnerving characteristics of his writing. To speak of a prose of vision is to speak equivocally, to speak not only of prose illuminated but of vision bedimmed. In too much of De Quincey's writing the visionary impulse is found awash in a sea of prose, prose written under anxiety to meet a printer's deadline and to please an undiscriminating periodical readership. Vision sinks into prose, becomes masked in chatter, details, the prosaic. Although his writings abundantly display persistent symbolic motifs and myth-like patterns of narrative, these elements remain too frequently elusive or recessive; they often emerge out of and fade back into the most incongruous of contexts, and they intermingle with material discursive in aim or indeed devoid of aim other than to fill up space in a magazine. Defying classification, these writings evade conventional yardsticks of criticism, and it is hardly surprising that they are so often relegated to that catch-all genre, the bane of nineteenth-century studies, 'non-fictional prose.' Given the enormous bulk of De Quincey's total work, his imagination is revealed clearly in but a few wholly satisfying works, such as the *Confessions of an English Opium-Eater*, *The English Mail-Coach*, and *Suspiria de Produndis*; more often it flares up in isolated passages or lurks obscurely beneath a prosaic surface. Prose such as this can offer no sharp boundaries between the 'discursive' and the 'imaginative,' but only varying degrees of imaginative intensification.

In attempting to deal with these problems I have allowed two assumptions to govern my procedure. First, I do not pretend to establish a defined 'canon' of works that may be classed as 'imaginative' as opposed to 'discursive.' I have selected for treatment works in which imaginative elements are predominant and salient or which otherwise aid in the exposition of important themes. In effect, this procedure has meant that not all the pieces I consider as eminently successful examples of De Quincey's prose art have been included, nor only these. Secondly, my commentaries treat the works considered as if they were in fact poems. Thus my central concern is with imagery and symbols, modulations of style and tone, and patterns of sequential ordering, as these elements operate upon one another to form a formal and thematic coherence. Discursive and other elements in these texts that take us away from what is imaginatively central are treated as peripheral. De Quincey is often prone to cloak his deepest imaginative concerns in expository disguises, thereby complicating the way we read him. Since his prose is ostensibly 'non-fictional,' we are sometimes lured away from the text of the *Confessions*, say, or of *Suspiria de Profundis*, into an extrinsic interest in the effects of opium or the traumas of the author's childhood, until we begin to think that the texts derive their importance from these interests when in fact the reverse is the case. I do not underestimate the biographical importance of these topics, but from my perspective they exist imagina-

tively in his works in the same way that the Abyssinian maid exists in
'Kubla Khan,' not as extrinsic agencies of inspiration but as part of the
autonomous universe of the works themselves. A similar point should be
made about De Quincey's portrayals of his dreams. Whatever form the
actual dreams may have taken, they are inaccessible except in the verbal
reconstructions in which we now receive them, tokens of a visionary
imagination embodied in words and subject to the same kind of literary
(as distinct from clinical) analysis that we find proper to apply to any
imaginative writing.

One area of interpretation deserves particular explanation in order to
forestall possible misunderstanding later on. Throughout his work, particularly the later writings, De Quincey asserts with forceful and sometimes tiresome iteration his adherence to orthodox Christian doctrine,
more or less Anglican in its colouring, and the figure of God appears
prominently in some of his best visionary writing. In treating this figure
in my interpretations I have allowed myself to be directed less by De
Quincey's assertions than by the imaginative logic of the works in which
the figure appears, and if God should appear in the following pages not
as a Christian deity but as an emblem of the artistic imagination, it is
because the pressure of the deep thematic argument in a given work, as I
read it, enforces this equation. I have even stressed at times, no doubt in
contradiction to what De Quincey would overtly avow as his creed, antinomian possibilities subversive to that creed. In so doing I am in part
attempting an exegesis that, to borrow a phrase from Geoffrey Hartman
in *Beyond Formalism* (New Haven 1970, p xiii), 'at some point, swerves
away from the literal sense of the text' so as to gain a liberating view of
what it might offer us. I do not believe, moreover, that this procedure is
unfaithful to De Quincey. His Christianity seems to be chiefly a matter of
ecclesiastical aestheticism, and, like that of many of his great Romantic
contemporaries, his imaginative work is filled with subversive question-
ings of received orthodoxies.

In considering the many ways in which De Quincey challenges our
interest as a man and as a writer I am acutely aware of how much this
study is forced to leave out. Yet De Quincey has received from competent
hands his due as a biographer, a critic, an anecdotalist, a stylist, an exponent of the effects of addiction, and it would be superfluous for me to
survey these concerns, though they sometimes touch upon my own. To
my greater regret I have avoided consideration of biographical data
which undoubtedly contributed to the moulding of De Quincey's imaginative outlook, and I have made sparing use of literary sources and

influences. Inclusion of such circumstantial material, however, would have made this a different kind of study. Good biographies exist, but detailed critical analyses of the major works have (with one or two exceptions) remained unattempted, and I have therefore felt obliged to remedy this neglect by making some of my own readings lengthy and detailed. No less is due a writer whose career exemplifies Romantic vision and forces that beset it and whose highest achievements transcend their precarious origins to make permanent claims on our interest.

This book has been published with the help of a grant from the Canadian Federation for the Humanities, using funds provided by the Social Sciences and Humanities Research Council of Canada, and a grant from the Andrew W. Mellon Foundation to the University of Toronto Press. I want to thank the Federation's Publications Committee for giving me attentive and useful appraisals of my work. A research leave granted by the University of Toronto enabled me to bring the manuscript to completion. A portion of the third chapter has previously appeared, in modified form, as 'De Quincey's "Knocking at the Gate in *Macbeth*": Dream and Prose Art' (*English Language Notes*, 3 [June 1976], 273–8); I am grateful to the editors of *English Language Notes* for their kind permission to reprint this material.

Although the body of critical and scholarly work devoted to De Quincey is relatively small, its quality is high and my debts to it run deep. Even where my aims and emphases have sometimes differed from theirs, the studies of such scholars and critics as Robert M. Adams, Albert Goldman, Alethea Hayter, John E. Jordan, Judson S. Lyon, J. Hillis Miller, François Moreux, and Edward Sackville West, as well as others cited in my notes, have proved indispensable to me. At a more general level (in so far as I can particularize debts so wide and so various) the insights of M.H. Abrams on the Romantic secularization of religious motifs, of Harold Bloom on the relation of Romantic vision to spiritual autonomy, and of Northrop Frye on the generic displacement of romance patterns and motifs have contributed valuably to the framework of critical assumptions in which I approach De Quincey's writings.

I owe a more specific and immediate debt of gratitude to A. Dwight Culler, who introduced me to De Quincey's imaginative writings in a graduate seminar at Yale and who subsequently watched over the early development of this study with unfailing encouragement and good advice. My friends and colleagues Richard Teleky, Tom Adamowski, Bob Bilan, and David Shaw, who have read the whole manuscript or varying portions of it, deserve many thanks for their thoughtful suggestions and

their timely prosecutions of my lapses. Jill Hannum, Bob Canavello, Iain
Glass, and Richard Bishop helped me considerably with proofreading
and other editorial chores at various stages in the progress of the manuscript towards final form. Jean C. Jamieson and Joan A. Bulger of the
University of Toronto Press gave counsel that was invariably enlighten-
ing. As for my typist, Mrs Jean Christie, any praise I could offer for her
skill, her patience, her good humour would sound excessive to those
unacquainted with her and still fall short of what she deserves. A simple
thanks will have to do.

Finally, for those to whom this book is dedicated, my parents, I wish I
had words adequate to express my debt of gratitude. It is a perpetual
source of sadness to me that my father, A. Michael De Luca, did not live
to see the completion of this work, which he inspired through his
encouragement and his lifelong devotion to humane scholarship.

Erindale College, University of Toronto, July 1979

ৠ[Texts and Abbreviations]ৡ

The standard edition of De Quincey's works is *The Collected Writings of Thomas De Quincey*, edited by David Masson, 14 volumes (Edinburgh: Adam and Charles Black 1889–90). All quotations from De Quincey except those specifically noted below or in my notes are taken from this edition and are cited in the text by volume and page number.

Quotations from the following works of De Quincey are cited in the text by the appropriate abbreviation and page number:

C   *The Confessions of an English Opium-Eater* (London: Taylor and Hessey 1822). This is the first edition of the original version of the *Confessions*.

D   *A Diary of Thomas De Quincey, 1803*, edited by Horace A. Eaton (London: Noel Douglas, n.d.)

SP   *Confessions of an English Opium-Eater and Suspiria de Profundis* (Boston: Ticknor, Reed, and Fields 1853). This volume contains the first reprint of the original *Blackwood's Edinburgh Magazine* series of the *Suspiria*: 57 (March, April, June 1845), 269–85, 489–502, 739–51; 58 (July 1845), 43–55.

THOMAS DE QUINCEY: THE PROSE OF VISION

❧[1]❧

'Impassioned Prose':
Myth and Expression

Like other imaginative writers imbued with the Romantic sensibility, De Quincey tends to make myths of his personal experience and his private speculations. Such myths are stories that attempt to make sense of our ordinary world and yet focus on a protagonist somehow privileged by visitations of a power not wholly of this world. In De Quincey's writings these stories are rarely explicit and their outlines seldom clear. Yet amid the immense variety of topics and styles in his work as a whole there appear certain figures, settings, and situations so gratuitously recurrent that one senses they really constitute the permanent imagery of some private world of experience.[1] In many of De Quincey's famous passages depicting heightened awareness or feeling the story of this private world, the outline of the myth, moves close to the surface, but the pervasive scattering of its characteristic imagery throughout his work suggests that the story scarcely confines itself to such passages. To discover the nature of the myth and its importance to De Quincey's most profound imaginative concerns one must seek for it as something inscribed grandly though obscurely in many works, unfolding in time as the writer refines his themes and his vision.

The place to begin such a search, however, is with the myth-like images themselves, particularly where they cluster in a concentrated way. Several such clusters appear in De Quincey's earliest surviving prose, in a context devoid of narrative elaboration or discursive exposition. They occur in a diary kept in the spring of 1803, his eighteenth year. The diary is very much the work of an introverted and precocious adolescent, absorbed in the prevalent literary fashions of Gothic and Oriental romance and filled with unrealized plans for additions to the genre, such as his 'Arabian Drama' which was to 'be an example of

Pathos and *Poetry* united, 'a feat he thought hitherto unaccomplished in literature (D 154–5). Despite these high ambitions there is not much evidence of any distinctive creative talent. The occasional fragments of romance invention to be found in De Quincey's diary are nevertheless valuable for anyone interested in the basic structure of the symbolic cosmos elaborated in his later writings, for these private jottings remain free of the distortions and displacements which the public status of the later work often occasioned. Sometimes single entries offer a mine of such material:

*Thursday morn*⁸*., May 5, 1803*
Last night I imagined to myself the heroine of the novel dying on an island of a lake, her chamber-windows (opening on a lawn) set wide open – and the sweet blooming roses breathing y^r. odours on her dying senses. One of my associations was derived from the *farm*. The morn⁸. of this event must be still – calm – balmy – beautifully blue etc. Another of my associa⁻ˢ. was a *Sunday* morning. Last night too I image myself looking through a glass. 'What do you see?' I see a man in the dim and shadowy perspective and (as it were) in a dream. He passes along in silence, and the hues of sorrow appear on his countenance. Who is he? 'A man darkly wonderful – above the beings of this world; but whether that shadow of him, which you saw, be y^e. shadow of a man long since passed away or of one yet hid in futurity, I may not tell you. There is something gloomily great in him; he wraps himself up in the dark recesses of his own soul; he looks over all mankind of all tongues – languages – and nations 'with an angel's ken'; ... I imaged too a banquet or carousel of feodal magnificence – such as in Schiller's Ghost-Seer, in y^e. middle of which a mysterious stranger should enter, on whose approach hangs fate and the dark roll of many woes, etc. I see Chatterton in the exceeding pain of death! in y^e. exhausted slumber of agony I see his arm weak as a child's – languid and faint in the extreme ... stretched out and raised at midnight – calling and pulling (faintly indeed but yet convulsively) some human breast to console him whom he had seen in the dreams of his fever'd soul.   (D 156–7)

A different entry, describing the plot of an intended poem, belongs imaginatively with these visions, especially the last:

A pathetic poem describing the emotions (strange and wild) of a man dying on a rock in the sea ... which he had swum to from a shipwreck ... within sight of his native cottage and his paternal hills.   (D 182)

One should not overestimate the importance of this mixture of adolescent fantasy and stock Gothic iconography, yet these images are to become for De Quincey more than fashionable draping for private emotion. Here the shadowy prototypes of the central figures in his imaginative life make their entrance, already playing varied roles designed to expose and exorcise dominating anxieties. The essential enemies are unnamed but clearly present, and the figures of Death and Life-in-Death from *The Ancient Mariner*, a work which the young De Quincey greatly admired, serve to represent them. Death here is, most simply, the intruder at the banquet, the thrust of horror upon the surface of life's abundance. The figure will reappear incessantly in De Quincey's later works in various guises – a mail-coach bearing down upon lovers in their frail gig, a murderer named Williams intruding upon happy and virtuous families, a sudden tidal influx driving deep into peaceful river valleys, described in the later version of the *Confessions* as the wrath of 'blind, unorganised nature' (III, 305). The confrontations present the horror of utter disjunction, the irreversible disruption of harmony and innocence. For its survivors the after-effect of this disjunction is Life-in-Death, the situation of the dying Chatterton, whose agony consists not so much in the terror of impending death but in the pains of his bitter experience and his hopeless yearning for a lost human comfort. The same motif is expressed spatially and more schematically in the instance of the shipwrecked man dying within sight of his native hills. Symbolic implications are close to the surface here; the rock is easily associated with the barren present of alienated Life-in-Death, the native landscape with a remembered pastoral innocence, and the sea which separates the two with the barren stretches of intervening disordered experience. The situation is a prototype of what some critics have seen as the paradigm of De Quincey's spiritual plight, the severance from an early bliss (the lost Ann of the *Confessions*, the lost Elizabeth of *Suspiria de Profundis*) and the immersion in a welter of harsh experience, later termed the 'Pariah Worlds,' expressed characteristically in imagery of labyrinthine cities, barren deserts, and chaotic voids.[2]

The other fantasies recorded in the diary entry of 5 May 1803 show, however, the presence of certain imaginative resources designed to mitigate the twin threats of Death and Life-in-Death and to circumvent their baleful influence. The scene of a heroine dying on an island in a lake represents the complementary opposite of the man dying on a rock in the sea. The lake is a ring of enchantment, sequestering death amid the profusions of a paradisal garden. There are certain perspectives, usually expressed in figures of enchanted groves, from which it seems to the Romantic imagination rich to die, where death appears not as a momentous intruder but as part of a larger and harmonious process of natural beauty, exemplified here by the failing breath of the girl which fades into the 'breathing' of the roses outside. Here death receives a glow of beauty by its interfusion with the symbols of blossoming nature, and life receives a quality of endless repose. De Quincey's later writings will often resort to this kind of enchanted region, in the several visions of dying children, their spirits assimilating with the dawn and the blue sky, in the persistent associations of death with summer, in the descriptions of lingering twilight, 'so sweet, so ghostly, in its soft golden smiles, silent as a dream, and quiet as the dying trance of a saint' (III, 344), or, to cite a more exotic variant, in the vision of the sunken city Savannah-la-Mar, which gives the impression of 'human life still subsisting in submarine asylums sacred from the storms that torment our upper air' (XIII, 360). These regions create a new kind of pastoral, a dream-pastoral extending its domain to both sides of the grave, making death a sanctuary from the anxieties that the knowledge of death originally caused.

To sublimate the terrors of that other enemy, Life-in-Death, is somewhat more difficult, but the rewards are more durable and significant. Sublimation becomes difficult because the victim of Life-in-Death suffers not just one momentous severance but repeated pains, and duration itself becomes an increasing torment as each moment widens the gap between the present moment and the primal loss. Even the creation of a dream-pastoral to assuage the pain of individual instances of loss demands a certain distancing from the event, a somewhat fragile poise of visionary perspective, but repeated personal trials tend to destroy that perspective or make it fitful. The victim of Life-in-Death, lacking real sanctuaries, must resort to the more desperate measure of envisioning his alienated and wandering existence as 'a life of allegory,' to use the apt phrase of Keats, that transforms the marks of his trials into emblems of an invisible glory. Hence the appearance of a man of sorrows in the diary entry, 'gloomily great,' is more than a Gothic indulgence if we view it in its proper relation to the other motifs which De Quincey has grouped with it. There is undoubtedly a certain amount of adolescent self-projection in the figure, but there is no confusion of identities. The man is visible only in a 'dim and shadowy perspective and (as it were) in a dream,' and his existence may be discovered only in past time or in futurity, in deep memories of mysterious provenance or in prophetic vision, but certainly not in the present of Life-in-Death. The figure is thus a prototype of what De Quincey will call in the *Suspiria de Profundis* 'the Dark Interpreter,' who is, he says, 'originally a mere reflex of my inner nature; ... but sometimes, as his face alters, his words alter; and they do not always seem such as I have used, or *could* use.[3] This figure is best described as the archetypal self which one constructs in dreams and visions, whose life mirrors that of the suffering individual but preserves an autonomy as well in a grander sphere of design.

Thus while the individual sufferer succumbs on his storm-tossed rock, the man of sorrows gains from his sufferings a god-like perspective of vision ('he looks over all mankind of all tongues – languages – and nations "with an angel's ken"'). The great endeavour of the individual sufferer is to search through the vicissitudes of his own life to discover some redemptive pattern that will assimilate it to the archetypal life of his vision. The best expression of a faith in such a pattern occurs in 'Levana and our Ladies of Sorrow,' where the Ladies reveal that De Quincey shall read in his sufferings 'elder truths, sad truths, grand truths, fearful truths. So shall he rise again *before* he dies. And so shall our commission be accomplished which from God we had – to plague his heart until we had unfolded the capacities of his spirit' (XIII, 369). Such a redemptive reading of personal experience is won with difficulty, however; hence De Quincey's continual writing and rewriting of his autobiography throughout his literary life in an effort to circle in upon the right embodiment of self-revelation.[4] Fifty years after his diary entries of 1803 he writes in the Preface to the Collected Edition of his works that he can think of no life-story properly told that would not 'fall within the reach of a deep, solemn, and sometimes even of a thrilling interest' (I, 10). Like the creation of the dream-pastoral, the recovery of the archetypal life also incorporates apparent misfortune into a larger and harmonious process, but it differs in the greater strength of its con-solation, for this is founded on a base of sorrows, not on their exclusion, on the promise of a gain in autonomous visionary power and not merely on the possibility of sanctuary.

These fragmentary samples of De Quincey's youthful imagination and the rapidly sketched lines of future development suggested as deriving from them should not be taken as exhausting the range of his fears or the imaginative and intellectual strategies which he will muster in order to emerge with satisfactory gains. One such strategy is available in the example of Wordsworth, who exalts man by commending him to nature, a procedure that attracts De Quincey right from the start, as two fer-vently worded drafts of a letter to the poet, copied in the diary, clearly suggest (D 167–8, 185–8). Later a training in metaphysics, tinged with the effects of opium, will bring a more rarified mode of consolation, a philosophy of dialectical progression 'resulting from mighty and equal antagonisms' (III, 395) and leading to the ultimate syntheses of apocalyptic vision. But the fantasies of De Quincey's diary establish for us some essential features of his literary art which any study of it must take into account. They give us the primal subject-matter, which oscillates between expression of the naked threats of experience and postulations of various imaginative compensations that diminish these threats. The diary also reveals the essential thematic pattern that he will restate, develop, and modify throughout the whole of his literary career. Baldly stated, De Quincey fears one kind of power, the external threat from an ultimate disjunctive force, and seeks to meet it with another power, his own visionary strength gathered in the face of experiential woe. He regrets one kind of loss, the death or disappearance of beloved objects known in a period of innocence, and seeks to replace it by evoking images of another kind of loss, loss of self in an easeful merging with a harmonious cosmos. Since the aspiration towards personal power and the aspiration towards a return to undifferentiated innocence are somewhat at odds, he will further seek to find visionary states in which the two goals become consubstantial. The history of his successes and failures in this search gives us the essential interest of his imaginative writings.

This thematic history is, however, finely interwoven with a different kind of history, comprising the successive verbal strategies employed to express urgent themes. Near the end of his writing career De Quincey tries to explain to the readers of his Collected Edition the nature of his most highly prized literary achievements. Some of his papers, he says, aim primarily to amuse but 'in doing so, may or may not happen to reach a higher station at which the amusement passes into an impassioned interest':

At times, the narrative rises into a far higher key. Most of all it does so at a period of the writer's life where, of necessity, a severe abstraction takes place from all that could invest him with any alien interest; ... nothing on the stage but a solitary infant, and its solitary combat with grief – a mighty darkness, and a sorrow without a voice. (I, 9)

The word 'impassioned' recurs a few pages later in a passage which is the necessary complement to the above:

Two remarks only I shall address to the equity of my reader. First, I desire to remind him of the perilous difficulty besieging all attempts to clothe in words

the visionary scenes derived from the world of dreams, where a single false
note, a single word in a wrong key, ruins the whole music; and, secondly, I
desire him to consider the utter sterility of universal literature in this one
department of impassioned prose. (I, 14)

Thus 'impassioned prose' supplies the voice lacking to the naked subject
of 'impassioned interest,' the child of woe in his primal experience of
severance, and the very principles which animate that voice provide a
countervailing emphasis against severance, for they depend upon the perfect gathering of many words, intricately interdependent. But De Quincey
is right to stress the difficulty of this gathering. Dreams are the 'art,' as it
were, of the unconscious, developing there unpredictably and swiftly
decaying in the memory; yet their emotional effect is like that of a 'whole
music,' which is the most consciously wrought and minutely organized
of all the arts. Language is normally too delimiting a medium to capture
the shifting lights of dream scenery, too gross a medium to attain the
refinements of music, and its capacities must be doubly strained if it attempts to simulate both. There is yet another difficulty; 'impassioned
prose' must compete with mere prose and the ready availability to a
journalist of too many things to say, too many lesser experiences to
recollect, too many temptations to 'amuse.' The chance of impassioned
utterance tends to lie buried in a rubble of words, just as the revelations
of dream imagery are so easily buried in the multiple distractions of ordinary life. To resurrect both utterance and revelation, and both together,
becomes the tortuous enterprise of De Quincey's career as an imaginative writer.[5]
   Although the project is tortuous, it contains for De Quincey peculiar
advantages as well as dangers. Always pressed to use his pen for quick
hire, he had scant leisure for pursuing the usual avenues of imaginative
literature – poetry, fiction, and drama – and, as is quite likely, had little
aptitude for them. The fantasies jotted down in his youthful diary may
provide some central images of his imaginative life, but he can do nothing
with these images alone, and the various literary projects which he
planned at eighteen remain unwritten. His first literary success as an
imaginative writer, the *Confessions of an English Opium-Eater*, curiously
coincides with his adoption of a career of popular journalism, and this
coincidence indicates how problematic his imaginative quest is likely to
be when it becomes translated into actual writing. If there is much
Romantic myth-making in De Quincey, expressed in impassioned prose,
the surrounding tissue of mere prose allows a strain of myth-breaking as
well, which the characteristics of nineteenth-century popular journalism

do little to thwart. For these characteristics can easily serve precisely the same functions as the displacement mechanisms of dreams according to Freudian analysis. If the burdened consciousness of the writer finds that the images welling from the deep centre of his imagination contain too much horror, or that the possibility of finding ultimate repose is too remote, or that the remaking of the self into a figure of visionary power is too arduous, then he can admit these concerns into his work only if they lose themselves in stretches of garrulity, anecdotal badinage, and pedantic digression.[6] If the imaginative centres of dream and vision pretend to penetrate the world of discursiveness or triviality in which they find themselves, they do so under a threat to their own bastions from an overwhelming surge of unimaginative details that seem to assert the primacy of the world of fact and the strong domination of daily experience as a round of inconsequence and incoherence.

Nevertheless De Quincey's journalistic traffic with the discursive and the trivial serves him as more than a defence against vision or an expression of scepticism. At the least, the very contrast in a given work between discursive thought and miscellanies of fact on the one hand and myth-making and vision on the other tends to show the latter to advantage. In a note to his piece 'System of the Heavens' (1846) De Quincey accurately describes the procedure found in many of his most interesting essays: 'from amongst the many relations of astronomy ... to select such as might allow of a solemn and impassioned, or a gay and playful, treatment. If, through the light torrent spray of fanciful images, ... the reader catches at intervals momentary glimpses of objects vast and awful in the rear, a much more impressive effect is likely to be obtained' (VIII, 8n). These glimpses, which he describes elsewhere as 'the half-sportive interlusory revealings of the symbolic' (I, 51), are impressive not only because they offer arresting juxtapositions of surface and depth but also because they hint at ultimate imaginings that are unnervingly close. Indeed everywhere in the 'light torrent spray' of De Quincey's more trivial effects lurk symbolic portents of his central imaginative experience, and any random event or image may prove a gate to recessive depths of revelation.[7] In works of mixed genre like the *Confessions* or *The English Mail-Coach* the concluding visions emerge out of a thick context of expository data, and these data cunningly hint at the visionary sublimity to come. It is an easy transition from this point to a sense that such data are the unacknowledged vehicles of the visionary powers, a justification of the inconsequential by the dictum that 'the least things in the universe must be secret mirrors to the greatest' (I, 129). De Quincey would readily assent to Wordsworth's announcement of 'higher minds' that 'build up greatest things from least suggestions,'[8] and indeed he and other prose writers of his generation profited from the Wordsworthian revolution of intermingling the low and the sublime, exposition and personal revelation, long before this practice became generally available to poets.[9] What from one perspective may seem to be an incompatible yoking of imaginative consciousness and reductive subject-matter can also appear from a different vantage-point as a blended and organic unity, pervasively expressive of the author's cherished themes.

In the following chapters I pursue through an analysis of specific works De Quincey's development throughout his career of the thematic concerns that emerge from his youthful fantasies. My analyses give particular stress to his clusters of recurrent symbolic imagery, those 'centres' which either expand their significance to pervade a work or which offer links to other centres. But this concern must be inseparable from an attention to form, to the stylistic and sequential elements that are intrinsic to the significance of the whole – the feints and dodges, the concealed revelations and revealed concealments, the bold alliances struck between materials of unlikely consort. In the *Confessions* we already find De Quincey a master of these strategies, and in the strategies we sense the working of a great and moving effort, an effort, in the face of and through instability (instability of form, subject-matter, and style, of powers of execution and outward circumstance), to claim a share in the illustrious strengths of the Romantic imagining power.

❧ 2 ❧

Confessions of an English
Opium-Eater, 1822

Few important literary works of the Romantic period have presented their fundamental preoccupations as diffidently or as obliquely as the *Confessions of an English Opium-Eater* of 1822. Even De Quincey's chief literary master, Wordsworth, offering *The Prelude* as no more than a versified review of his capacities for writing a major poem, manages to launch the review with submerged invocations of a naturalized muse ('there is a blessing in this gentle breeze') and allusions to Milton ('the earth is all before me' I, 1, 14), so that large pretensions are implicit from the outset. Although scarcely devoid of Wordsworthian influence, the *Confessions* purports to be nothing more than instructive journalism, claiming no special attention undeserved by other anonymous contributions to the *London Magazine* in late 1821. Throughout the work there is a pervasive tendency to externalize, often reductively, the data of inward experience, a tendency to reduce this experience to a case-history of pharmaceutical effects. Near the end of the work De Quincey insists that 'the interest of the judicious reader will not attach itself chiefly to the subject of the fascinating spells, but to the fascinating power. Not the opium-eater, but the opium, is the true hero of the tale; and the legitimate centre on which the interest revolves. The object was to display the marvellous agency of opium, whether for pleasure or for pain: if that is done, the action of the piece has closed' (C 180–1). He offers the narrative of incidents in Wales and London following his flight from school, not for its own sake, but to 'furnish the key' to some of the opium-dreams. The life and the opium-eating are thus related only in the most casual way; the author first takes opium to relieve a toothache and some years later becomes addicted from an increased dosage designed to relieve a stomach ailment. Deeper connections between the personality presented in this work and the addiction remain covert.

The frequent occurrence of cadenzas of elevated prose no doubt counteracts these reductive tendencies and calls attention to the work as no ordinary case-history. It is not easy to determine, however, what makes the book unusual aside from its patches of verbal felicity, and attempts to trace the sources of the emotional power in these felicitous passages encounter the problem of a narrative which seems to veer throughout towards inconsequence and then towards momentous revelation without ever quite arriving at either point. Several peculiarities of presentation collaborate to create this effect. The narration, for example, is episodic, consisting largely of brief and unsensational encounters or even shadings of mood in static situations. There are, moreover, curious proportions of emphasis, so that crucially formative periods in the boy's life, such as his trials with schoolmasters and guardians and his decision to run away, receive a hasty summary in a page or two, whereas certain recollected moments of the actual leave-taking rivet the writer's attention: the expression of the headmaster and of a portrait on the wall, the weather, the accidental clatter of a trunk down a flight of stairs. In many episodes trivial occurrences generate unexpected plangencies, although at least one obvious centre of emotional interest, De Quincey's relation with Ann of Oxford Street, receives a parsimonious allotment of space amid sometimes tedious accounts of his financial preoccupations. The whole work is also marked by discontinuities of a suspect nature, as if presumed emotional connectives were suppressed, most notably in the transition from the end of the 'Preliminary Confessions,' with its intense expression of separation from loving female figures, to the beginning of 'The Pleasures of Opium,' where we find the hero purchasing opium for his toothache; and the opium-reveries themselves, wrought with careful artistry, finally emerge more or less detached from preceding sections, the stated connections being only of the most cursory sort.

These oblique and unpredictable procedures, like the displacement techniques of dreams, keep the contours of the work's inner life at some distance below its shifting surface and yield them to the interpreter only in resonant juxtapositions and in the aggregate of accumulated episodes, where recurrent patterns become discernible. Unlike the later version of the *Confessions* or the 'spots of time' in Wordsworth's *Prelude*, the episodes of the *Confessions* of 1822 never contain their own discursive interpretation. Some, however, are transparent in their symbolic intent and provide guides for following De Quincey's elusive path of revelation. One such episode in the 'Preliminary Confessions,' briefly cited above, occurs at the moment of De Quincey's departure from school, and it radiates significant implications not only upon the incidents which surround it but also upon the work as a whole:

I dressed myself, took my hat and gloves, and lingered a little in the room. For the last year and a half this room had been my 'pensive citadel:' here I had read and studied through all the hours of night: and though true it was, that for the latter part of this time I, who was framed for love and gentle affections, had lost my gaiety and happiness, during the strife and fever of contention with my guardian; yet, on the other hand, as a boy, so passionately fond of books, and dedicated to intellectual pursuits, I could not fail to have enjoyed many happy hours in the midst of general dejection. I wept as I looked round on the chair, hearth, writing-table, and other familiar objects, knowing too certainly, that I looked upon them for the last time. Whilst I write this, it is eighteen years ago: and yet, at this moment, I see distinctly as if it were yesterday, the lineaments and expression of the object on which I fixed my parting gaze: it was a picture of the lovely ———, which hung over the mantelpiece; the eyes and mouth of which were so beautiful, and the whole countenance so radiant with benignity and divine tranquillity, that I had a thousand times laid down my pen, or my book, to gather consolation from it, as a devotee from his patron saint. Whilst I was yet gazing upon it, the deep tones of —— clock proclaimed that it was four o'clock. I went up to the picture, kissed it, and then gently walked out, and closed the door for ever! (C 22–3)

This passage is worth pausing over, because it contains the first point of emotional quickening in the book. There is nothing unusual in the boy's valedictory sadness as he surveys 'the chair, hearth, writing-table, and other familiar objects' for the last time, since even despised places commonly generate nostalgia in moments such as this. Far more striking is his rhapsody over the portrait on his wall (an unknown lady of the seventeenth century, as we learn from the second version of the *Confessions*.) The emotion is so far in excess of the object described that the fact becomes a point of attention in itself.

Two apparently contradictory impressions are likely to emerge from this rhapsody; first, that the portrait represents a palpable presence of divine consolation radiating the 'benignity' and 'divine tranquility' of a 'patron saint,' a presence which maintains such clarity in the mind over the gap of eighteen years that it suggests a heavenly visitation as much as it does an icon; secondly, that the picture scarcely exists at all as an object of real interest, that it is the creature of De Quincey's need (both as fugitive schoolboy and as author of the *Confessions*) to find an external emblem that will serve him, 'framed for love and gentle affections,' as a radiant reflector of these passions. Whatever clarity the lineaments of the portrait have for De Quincey, they are obscured for the reader by the effulgence of the passion; the picture is abruptly introduced into the narrative and receives no further reference; the lady is unknown (a point accentuated by De Quincey's concealing dashes, part of an attempt to maintain the anonymity of the work). Reversing the usual characteristics of dreams and of much symbolist writing, the significant emotion expressed is obvious and salient, the formal symbol recessive and unclear.

De Quincey chooses to launch his narrative therefore with a vision of ideality virtually unencumbered by the compromises imposed by embodiment in the tangible forms of daily life. The lady in the portrait is divine precisely because she is explicitly an emblem and therefore a source of uncontingent solace, like the memory-landscapes that flash upon the inward eye in Wordsworth's poetry. As the work progresses, this ideality accommodates itself increasingly to three-dimensional human figures, most notably De Quincey's wife Margaret and Ann of Oxford Street. This accommodation provides a vitality to the vision, more richly satisfying to human needs than an arbitrary radiance emanating from an emblematic space can be, but it also exposes the vision to all the contingencies of mutable existence. For the time being, however, the act of faith of which the portrait is an external token maintains its sway and, having enabled the boy to endure during his crises at school, it also allows him to close the door on that experience in exchange for the possible crises of unknown experience ahead.

The benevolence epitomized in the portrait clothes another vignette from the scenes of departure in an ameliorative light not intrinsic to the situation. On the evening before he flees De Quincey confronts another visage quite different from the unknown lovely lady's, that of the old headmaster, whose stultifying ways have prompted the boy's decision to flee in the first place:

I bowed to him, and looked earnestly in his face, thinking to myself, 'He is old and infirm, and in this world I shall not see him again.' I was right: I never *did* see him again, nor ever shall. He looked at me complacently, smiled good-naturedly, returned my salutation (or rather, my valediction), and we parted (though he knew it not) for ever. I could not reverence him intellectually: but he had been uniformly kind to me, and had allowed me many indulgences: and I grieved at the thought of the mortification I should inflict upon him. (C 20)

This is the same man who, a few pages earlier, is called 'coarse, clumsy, and inelegant' and who 'could not disguise from my hourly notice, the poverty and meagreness of his understanding' (C 16), the man solely responsible for the boy's decision to flee. A psychological reading of this relationship between master and pupil would find in it the usual conflict of the generations, the rebellion against the father-figure. There is no sense of this conflict, however, in De Quincey's account. The earnest gaze into the old man's face reveals nothing but benignity, and just as the boy imagines the headmaster's pain when he learns of the errant child, so does the passage reveal a genuine pain at the prospective loss of the elder. In this way even the face of obstructive authority becomes assimilated into the circle of benign presences of which the portrait is the prototype.

The same kind of softening grace spreads its influence more discreetly throughout the narrative, rendering muted or harmless what otherwise might be painful confrontations or foreboding portents. Bold assertion and fear, complementary alternatives of emotion accompanying most adult action in the world of experience, are subdued in their expression here. De Quincey does say of his decision to run away that 'I was firm and immoveable in my purpose: but yet agitated by anticipation of uncertain danger and troubles' (C 21), but there is no insistence on these cross-currents of emotion such as we find so pervasively in the later version of the *Confessions*. The mood of the 'Preliminary Confessions' has its closest analogue in Blake's *Songs of Innocence*, which, like De Quincey's work, include the sufferings of urban experience without acknowledgment of repressive attitudes as the cause of these sufferings or of rebellion as the appropriate response. In the *Songs* every trial is alleviated by more than adequate consolation, sometimes even brought about by a transformation of the agent of suffering into an agent of redemption.[1] Whatever his knowledge of Blake may have been, De Quincey presents us with a demythologized version of the same process. He does not pass over his suffering, indeed he gives a rather excessive estimate of its intensity (his hunger in London, he says, was 'as bitter, perhaps, as ever any human being can have suffered who has survived it' (C 37), but the sufferings are a matter of flat assertion, whereas the actual anecdotes record a succession of mitigations, of timely hospitalities, rescues, and unexpected acts of good will. Wandering on little sustenance in Wales, De Quincey receives unstinting hospitality from a whole family of young cottagers; in London, where he is starving, a disreputable lawyer provides meagre lodgings and food; when the youth is fainting from weakness on Oxford Street, Ann, the saintly prostitute, fetches providentially restorative wine; an initially surly coach passenger comforts him on the way to Eton when he learns of the youth's plight; and young Lord Desart at Eton, imitating Ann of Oxford Street on a higher social plane, provides more sustaining wine. Each of these incidents is trivial in itself, but in the aggregate they compose an unmistakable pattern of inevitable respites to possible suffering.

This faith in the ready presence of love converts the state of experience into an enlargement of the state of innocence. The chief characteristic of this state, aside from its provision of rescue from impending disasters, is its postulation of a community of acceptance and mutual generosity that persists despite circumstances of external suffering. This community seems to reconstitute itself in a variety of social levels and physical situations. Nor is it entirely a one-sided flow of hospitality, of which the youth is the perpetual beneficiary. To a forlorn child who also lodges in the lawyer's house De Quincey himself assumes a protective role: 'We lay upon the floor, with a bundle of cursed law papers for a pillow: but with no other covering than a sort of large horseman's cloak: ... The poor child crept close to me for warmth, and for security against her ghostly enemies. When I was not more than usually ill, I took her into my arms, so that, in general, she was tolerably warm, and often slept when I could not' (C 39). This episode captures some of the spirit of Blake's 'Chimney Sweeper,' in which the speaker, himself a suffering innocent, acquires through his innocence a paternal role.

The most imaginatively fulfilled example of this communal relation in the *Confessions* is the famous episode of Ann of Oxford Street. In her relation to De Quincey Ann embodies aspects of mother, child, and lover. Forced into prostitution by a swindler who made off with her property, she is also a wandering innocent. Since she is younger than De Quincey and uneducated, he is able to help her by trying to obtain legal redress for the injustices done to her (C 49), just as he performs simpler acts of generosity for the forsaken child. But in another sense his relation to Ann is the reverse of his relation to the child, for Ann's prostitution has inured her to the role of outcast in a hostile world of experience, so that she is able to bring protective comfort when he finds his own hardships unendurable:

I had been leaning my head against her bosom; and all at once I sank from her arms and fell backwards on the steps. From the sensations I then had, I felt an inner conviction of the liveliest kind that without some powerful and reviving stimulus, I should either have died on the spot – or should at least have sunk to a point of exhaustion from which all re-ascent under my friendless circumstances would soon have become hopeless. Then it was, at this crisis of my fate, that my poor orphan companion – who had herself met with little but injuries in this world – stretched out a saving hand to me. Uttering a cry of terror, but without a moment's delay, she ran off into Oxford-street, and in less time than could be imagined, returned to me with a glass of port wine and spices, that acted upon my empty stomach (which at that time would have rejected all solid food) with an instantaneous power of restoration ... (c 50–1)

De Quincey goes on, in an extravagant apostrophe to Ann, to speak of his 'perfect love' (c 51) for her and of a 'heart oppressed with gratitude' (c 52). These sentiments would seem disproportionate to the trivial event in Oxford Street if the language describing the event did not suggest that his imagination has assimilated it into his world of emblems. The references to impending death, to a 'crisis in my fate,' to sinking and 're-ascent,' and to the almost miraculous restorative power of wine introduce symbolic resonances in an otherwise prosaic description. Physical exhaustion can thus become a correlative of a psychic defeat in the world of experience, the gift of wine a sacramental correlative of a love that preserves and renews the community of innocence.

Visually the tableau of a ministering woman bent over the prostrate form of her beloved suggests the iconography of the Pietà, while the offering of wine suggests christological associations of a different sort (De Quincey speaks of Ann a few pages later as 'the saviour of my life,' c 62), so that these associations are delicately distributed to each participant in the scene. In effect, divine love is made to inhere in situations of mutual reciprocity, just as the emblems of sacred events are accommodated to the quotidian of Oxford Street. In the visage of Ann De Quincey finds the embodied fulfilment of the promise of love offered by the portrait in his room at school. That earlier scene shows an outpouring of love, nominally assigned to a lovely lady of almost divine station but actually radiating so intensely from the devotee's desires that it virtually obliterates the lineaments of the emblem that quickened it. With Ann love becomes mutual, a human sharing, realized in a distinct act of efficacious giving, and made tangible by its manifestation in a London street.

The whole of the 'Preliminary Confessions' shows a development from a primary awakening of unspecified love and a faith in its more than adequate return, to a partial fulfilment of these qualities in a number of encounters within ordinary experience, and finally to a rooting of the love and a ratification of the faith in a special individual. Paradoxically, however, this accommodation of the principles of the state of innocence to a relation between two people contains seeds of destruction for that state. When De Quincey leaves the portrait behind in his flight from school he does not leave his innocence, for he has lost the physical presence of what is only an emblem, but this innocence cannot sustain the loss of love concentrated and embodied in a living human presence. When Ann disappears shortly after her act of generosity, the community of love shatters. Although De Quincey will go on to find other comforters and other comforts, they will not obliterate his sense of unmitigatable loss, of loneliness, and of futile search. It is significant that upon Ann's disappearance the note of these sorrows enters into the *Confessions*:

To this hour, I have never heard a syllable about her. This, amongst such troubles as most men meet with in this life, has been my heaviest affliction. – If she lived, doubtless we must have been sometimes in search of each other, at the very same moment, through the mighty labyrinths of London; perhaps even within a few feet of each other – a barrier no wider in a London street, often amounting in the end to a separation for eternity! During some years, I hoped that she *did* live; and I suppose that, in the literal and unrhetorical use of the word *myriad*, I may say that on my different visits to London, I have looked into many, many myriads of female faces, in the hope of meeting her. (c 78)

It is a measure of its symbolic import that after years of intervening misery, of poverty and opium addiction, De Quincey can call the loss of this brief acquaintance with a London street girl his 'heaviest affliction.' Its heaviness consists in the conversion of the characteristics of innocence to those of experience. The subject becomes an isolated self, for the children of suffering no longer come together in a community of love but wander fruitlessly through a labyrinth. Proximity is no guarantee of restoration, because in such an environment any separation, even of a few feet, is an immeasurable gap. Encounters, although 'myriad,' fail to produce communal feelings, for the seeker finds only multiplications of faces, none of them the right face. The ending of the 'Preliminary Confessions' sets the seal upon this departure from innocence, as De Quincey considers his situation at the moment of actual writing, a life of hardship in London once again and separation from his home and his wife Margaret, a successor to Ann. Contemplating these remote solaces, he concludes the first section of the book with a cry: 'That way I would fly for comfort' (C 86).

After this plaintive cry the bold heading of the second section, 'The Pleasures of Opium,' suggests that substitute refuges are available. Although De Quincey resolutely avoids associating his turning to opium with the loss of a sustaining love, the disposition of his reminiscences in such a way as to juxtapose these dominating concerns suggests a covert linkage of them in his imagination. At any rate, his description of his first purchase of the drug has a peculiar familiarity. Suffering this time 'excruciating rheumatic pains of the head and face' (C 87), De Quincey resorts to an apothecary who, upon supplying him with the drug, becomes an 'unconscious minister of celestial pleasures,' the 'beatific vision of an immortal druggist' (C 88).

But unlike Ann, who suggests divinity because of her love and whose gift of wine acquires symbolic importance as a token of that love, the druggist is 'beatific' by courtesy only and his elixir signifies nothing more than itself. Opium may provide physical relief and raptures of vision, but it cannot restore the community of human love, the hallmark of the innocent state. In the second half of the Confessions the focus shifts away from depictions of human encounters and responsive gestures and towards depictions of the autonomous mental states, whether beatific or terrifying, of an isolated individual. Although De Quincey may often speak as if opium were his divinity and his beloved, the drug is neither, for it offers no salvation from the isolation of the self, but merely mirrors back in more intense form the range of potentialities inherent in the situation of a subject who has departed from the early world of a loving community. From this point of view opium serves, like the author's unremitting succession of ill-defined but excruciating ailments, to externalize a history of the spirit, deceiving some readers into regarding the book as a medical case-history, and perhaps deceiving De Quincey himself, who continually yields to this exterior influence the sole credit for effects which are in fact self-created and self-directed.

To read the Confessions as a case-history of course in no way violates the work, nor is it inappropriate to read it as a kind of moral allegory, in which the hero, missing real human love, resorts to a deceptive haven that eventually becomes his prison.[2] The second reading, with its stress on a sinister equivocation, represented by the section titles 'The Pleasures of Opium' and 'The Pains of Opium,' comes closer to the imaginative substratum of the book, but it still concentrates its focus on the powers of a nominal agent, opium, rather than upon the pattern of psychic content which the opium-visions reveal. I prefer a reading that integrates the *Confessions* with the fundamental thematic concerns of De Quincey's imaginative work in general, concerns which centre upon the situation of the solitary individual in a post-lapsarian state of lost community. In such a reading the importance of opium consists in providing special perspectives on the alternative states open to such an individual by clarifying the configurations of these states with a visionary simplicity rarely available to more sober perception.

Of these alternatives, the first, which is embodied in 'The Pleasures of Opium,' involves a state of creative autonomy, a 'higher innocence' that transcends the kind of innocence depicted in the 'Preliminary Confessions,' dependent on a faith in unfailing external benevolences. It appears that one possible consequence of the loss of community is an opportunity for the individual mind to expand freely in the vacated space, so that it eventually contains its own ordered cosmos. When opium first opens the doors of perception for De Quincey, it offers revelations of the self: 'oh! heavens! what a revulsion! what an upheaving, from its lowest depths, of the inner spirit! what an apocalypse of the world within me!' (c 90). The mind is its own place and does not need another world, but, as other anecdotes in 'The Pleasures of Opium' show, De Quincey's imagination can freely integrate the world around him into a harmonious vision, drawing the heterogeneous into an encompassing pattern of the mind's acts and its possessions.

This process of integration operates in several dimensions, both spatial and temporal, in modes of exterior sensation and inward reflection. Describing how opium influences his response to music, De Quincey notes that 'a chorus, &c. of elaborate harmony, displayed before me, as in a piece of arras work, the whole of my past life – not as if recalled by an act of memory, but as if present and incarnated in the music: no longer painful to dwell upon: but the detail of its incidents removed, or blended in some hazy abstraction; and its passions exalted, spiritualized, and sublimed' (c 106). Here the imagination attempts a complex synthesis, reaching inward to recapture the lost moments of the listener's past and outward to capture the music so as to make it an inner music of the personal history; past and present, subject and object fuse in a presence that transcends its disparate elements. But the imagination does not need such refined pleasures as music to accomplish these effects. After discovering opium De Quincey returns continually to the streets of London, the scene of his early sufferings and of his love, to find that even as a wandering solitary he can encompass the multiplicity of the city's parts and its human throngs. Threading like a fearless discoverer through a labyrinth of streets, casually joining in the social gatherings of the poor, attending theatres (C 110–11) or seeking out 'solitude and silence' (C 112), he makes all environments his own, fulfilling the Miltonic ideal, explicitly suggested in a reference to 'L'Allegro' and 'Il Penseroso' (C 91), of the man who can mingle participation in experience and an aloofness from that experience in a serene balance.

At the height of such expansion of individual consciousness there occurs a kind of inversion of empirical perspectives in which the observing mind becomes the encompassing circumference of the world of objects, and the world pales into an emblem of the mind's autonomy. The most memorable expression of this inversion in the *Confessions* occurs in De Quincey's description of the scenic panorama of Liverpool harbour as observed in a drug-induced reverie:

And more than once it has happened to me, on a summer night, when I have been at an open window, in a room from which I could overlook the sea at a mile below me, and could command a view of the great town of L——, at about the same distance, that I have sat, from sun-set to sun-rise, motionless, and without wishing to move.

I shall be charged with mysticism, Behmenism, quietism, &c. but *that* shall not alarm me ... I say, then, that it has often struck me that the scene itself was somewhat typical of what took place in such a reverie. The town of L—— represented the earth, with its sorrows and its graves left behind, yet not out of sight, nor wholly forgotten. The ocean, in everlasting but gentle agitation, and brooded over by dove-like calm, might not unfitly typify the mind and the mood which then swayed it. For it seemed to me as if then first I stood at a distance, and aloof from the uproar of life; as if the tumult, the fever, and the strife, were suspended; a respite granted from the secret burthens of the heart; a sabbath of repose; a resting from human labours. Here were the hopes which blossomed in the paths of life, reconciled with the peace which is in the grave; motions of the intellect as unwearied as the heavens, yet for all anxieties a halcyon calm: a tranquillity that seemed no product of inertia, but as if resulting from mighty and equal antagonisms; infinite activities, infinite repose. (C 113–14)

This description has the force of an epiphany within the work, a centre of concentrated value, for it incorporates the vision of innocence, a generous community of reciprocity, into the vision of higher innocence, the exaltation of mind over sense. The reciprocity derives from a relation between observer and scene in which each participant exchanges attributes proper to the other: the motionless observer loses consciousness of self and acquires the fixities of a landscape, and the scene acquires a human complexity as a dwelling-place of memory, emotion, and intellect. In this exchange of attributes there is a kind of depersonalized revival of De Quincey's relation to Ann.

At the same time, however, the passage exalts the observer far above the scene. Like the archetypal figure in the diary of 1803 who 'looks over all mankind of all tongues – languages – and nations "with an angel's ken",' De Quincey surveys the whole world, by proxy as it were, in its synechdocal emblems of city and sea. But there is another, more important kind of exaltation, for the visible scene has become 'typical' of the reverie, a mirror of the mind observing it, so that the objective world serves to proclaim the grandeur of the subjective. This mirroring proves, on analysis, to be quite precise. The town plainly represents the memory of loss, 'its sorrows and its graves left behind, yet not out of sight, nor wholly forgotten,' whereas the sea represents the redeeming power of the imaginative solitary, a dialectic play of the intellect which offers repose to its own energies, harmony to its own created multiplicities. The figure of the sea as a type of the mind recalls Marvell's reference in 'The Garden' to

> The Mind, that Ocean where each kind
> Does streight its own resemblance find;[3]

and the progress of the soul to a state of autonomy depicted in that poem accords well with the traditions of Christian mysticism to which De Quincey explicitly alludes in this passage. The city, the domain of unforgotten severances, yields pre-eminence to the sea, the domain of perpetual renewal and completion, as emotional experience yields pre-eminence to the autonomous intellect. The traditional end-point of this progress, the consummation of the individual intellect in that of God, is, however, averted here. The significance of the vision resides in its relevance to a human beholder, who contemplates equally the intellectual balance of repose and activity and the unforgotten sorrows of experience.

This visionary synthesis so retentive of human dimensions owes less to orthodox or esoteric traditions than it does to Wordsworth, whose meditation on Mt Snowdon as described in *The Prelude* of 1805 probably provides the closest source for the description of Liverpool harbour.[4] Here too a dialectic of complementary components within the observed scene creates a synthesis in which the scene becomes a reflexive emblem of the mind observing it:

> A meditation rose in me that night
> Upon the lonely Mountain when the scene
> Had pass'd away, and it appear'd to me
> The perfect image of a mighty Mind,
> Of one that feeds upon infinity ... (XIII [1805], 66-70)

This passage relates to several phrases from De Quincey's description of Liverpool harbour: 'the scene itself was typical of what took place in such a reverie,' 'the ocean ... might not unfitly typify the mind,' 'infinite activities, infinite repose.' Although De Quincey offers a more hieratic set of emblems than we find in *The Prelude* of 1805 and puts more rhetorical stress on the ultimate value of repose, Liverpool harbour remains the most eloquent expression in De Quincey's writings of that Wordsworthian faith in a secular and internalized centre of transcendence.

When the first world of communal innocence departs, one needs a certain strength to maintain the faith that an expansion of autonomous imaginative powers, such as 'The Pleasures of Opium' describes, will inevitably succeed it. If the strength fails, the sense of loss becomes paramount and the alternative reign of Life-in-Death begins. The influence of Coleridge presides in 'The Pains of Opium,' as the influence of Wordsworth has done in 'The Pleasures,' and his equivocal maxim in the 'Dejection' ode – 'We receive but what we give' – would provide an appropriate epigraph for this section of the work. The essence of the pains resides not in the lurid excesses of nightmare vision but in the sense of personal incapacity to regain the lost community or to reintegrate the phenomena of a limitless externality into a harmonious vision. Like the hero of the 'Dejection' ode, the figure who wanders through these alienating landscapes suffers from a maimed will and a maddening consciousness of his predicament, a consciousness that breeds further incapacity.

The remarkable fantasia on Piranesi's engravings of dream-prisons provides an excellent starting-point for discussion of the section, for no passage in the work captures the theme of futility more succinctly. Although De Quincey never saw the engravings and derived his passage from a description supplied, appropriately enough, by Coleridge, he manages to capture the same odd combination of ordered repetition and proliferating incoherence for which the engravings are notable:

Creeping along the sides of the walls, you perceived a staircase; and upon it, groping his way upwards, was Piranesi himself: follow the stairs a little further and you perceive it to come to a sudden abrupt termination, without any balustrade, and allowing no step onwards to him who had reached the extremity, except into the depths below. Whatever is to become of poor Piranesi, you suppose, at least, that his labours must in some way terminate here. But raise your eyes, and behold a second flight of stairs still higher; on which again Piranesi is perceived, but this time standing on the very brink of the abyss. Again elevate your eye, and a still more aerial flight of stairs is beheld: and again is poor Piranesi busy on his aspiring labours: and so on, until the unfinished stairs and Piranesi both are lost in the upper gloom of the hall. (c 163–4)

Piranesi's labours provide a savage parody of the earlier vision of 'infinite activities, infinite repose' contained in the reverie on Liverpool harbour. Stretching behind Piranesi, flight after flight, is the stony record of his wearied activity in a world emptied of meaningful forms and ahead of him is the 'infinite repose' of abrupt annihilation in the abyss.[5] Although the threat of immediate and ultimate disaster is directly before him, the next step he takes proves only to extend the staircase of his infinitely repeated labours this side of the abyss; he is able neither to quit one horror nor to banish the vision of the other.

As De Quincey presents him, Piranesi seems like a character displaced from some twentieth-century delineation of the existential abyss, absurd in the diligence with which he pursues his climb towards new heights of hopelessness. Other passages from 'The Pains of Opium,' however, describe a more characteristically Romantic plight, dejection over lost intellectual powers, and thus add a dimension of moral pathos to the stark absurdity of the condition which Piranesi exemplifies. One such passage describes a debilitating inertia that prevents De Quincey from completing a grand work of philosophical synthesis:

I had devoted the labour of my whole life, and had dedicated my intellect, blossoms and fruits, to the slow and elaborate toil of constructing one single work, to which I presumed to give the title of an unfinished work of Spinosa's; viz. *De emendatione humani intellectûs*. This was now lying locked up, as by frost, like any Spanish bridge or aqueduct, begun upon too great a scale for the resources of the architect; and, instead of surviving me as a monument of wishes at least, and aspirations, and a life of labour dedicated to the exalta-tion of human nature in that way in which God had best fitted me to pro-mote so great an object, it was likely to stand a memorial to my children of hopes defeated, of baffled efforts, of materials uselessly accumulated, of foun-dations laid that were never to support a superstructure, – of the grief and the ruin of the architect. (c 149)

It is a powerful passage, one of the few in the work that really sounds like a 'confession' and not the disguise of one. The great philosophical project 'dedicated to the exaltation of human nature' was intended to provide a counterpart in moral, intellectual, and social spheres to that transcendent synthesis achieved in the private apotheosis at Liverpool harbour. But here the intellect does not expand to cosmic proportions; the self shrinks away, rather, amid an expanding world of unyielding objects, so that there is nothing left but a sense of 'infantine feebleness' (c 149) that makes every project a monument to incapacity. De Quincey's architectural metaphors recall Piranesi's engravings, and there is not really much difference between Piranesi's labours as depicted in De Quincey's fantasia and his own failure to complete *De emendatione humani intellectûs*. Although Piranesi perseveres at his nameless project while De Quincey does not, both are the architects of ruins. The highest step on the impressive flights of stairs leads not to some portentous threshold that gives a rationale to the whole but only to a yawning void. If the power to bridge that void is lacking, then the sum of one's previous labours, however impressive, is bound to remain 'a memorial ... of hopes defeated, of baffled efforts, of materials uselessly accumulated, of founda-tions laid that were never to support a superstructure.' The existential abyss is objectively horrid to contemplate, but the core of the architect's suffering derives from the consciousness of failure to supply the vital connection between subject and object that will restore a humanistic shape to his world.

After a somewhat dilatory and episodic 'Introduction to the Pains of Opium,' which produces an effect, peculiarly appropriate to the emerging theme, of much scurrying without any advancement to the goal, De

Quincey finally brings together the motifs of the work in a dark visionary finale remarkable for its formidable displays of thematic concentration and stylistic power. This finale consists of four cycles of dream-visions, each presenting a different paradigm of the dreamer's spiritual condition and his attempts to respond to it. In the first and third various attempts at imaginative integration decay before the dreamer's eyes; the second depicts what appears to be a desperate response to these failures of integration, a retreat into paranoia; and the fourth represents a kind of apocalyptic synthesis of the preceding visions. Because of their symbolic density these dream-visions demand a more detailed consecutive commentary than has been necessary so far.

The imagination often attempts to cope with threats of incoherence and disjunction by creating counter-worlds that either promise a triumphant victory over the uncertainties of experience or absorb bitter truths into a harmony of acceptance. Of the first kind is the vision of apocalypse, the sight of that New Jerusalem where all contraries are united without vitiation of their independent powers, where proliferating energy and beauty are one. Wordsworth saw in the dialectic of natural contraries in Simplon Pass the 'characters of the great Apocalypse,' and it is significant that De Quincey should quote as something that might, he says, 'have been copied from my architectural dreams' (C 165) a passage from *The Excursion*, where the forms of nature, clouds and evening sky, evolve into a precise resemblance of the traditional Celestial City:

> The appearance, instantaneously disclosed,
> Was of a mighty city – boldly say
> A wilderness of building, sinking far
> And self-withdrawn into a wondrous depth,
> Far sinking into splendour – without end!
> Fabric it seem'd of diamond, and of gold,
> With alabaster domes, and silver spires,
> And blazing terrace upon terrace, high
> Uplifted; here, serene pavilions bright
> In avenues disposed; there towers begirt
> With battlements that on their restless fronts
> Bore stars – illumination of all gems!   (C 165)[6]

Wordsworth's persona for the alienated self, the Solitary, goes on to claim how this scene became for him an emblem of renewed faith, for it was 'such as by Hebrew Prophets were beheld in vision,' 'the revealed abode of Spirits in beatitude.'[7] De Quincey, however, does not extend his quotation to include these assertions of faith. Lacking the guarantee of divine control, the image hints, for all its glamour, at a dangerous instability, at precious metals and stones that are only vapours, at a building that is also a 'wilderness' and battlements that are 'restless,' all 'sinking far' into, incalculable, recessive depths. An imagination that hopes to find refuge in the energetic warfare of contraries must be capable of supplying glorious lighting effects to this surging mass to turn it into a unified image of apocalyptic beauty.

The sequence of dreams moves, however, in the opposite direction. As if the clouds that composed the vision of splendour have somehow condensed, De Quincey's dreams lose their architectural character and begin to depict 'translucent lakes, shining like mirrors' (C 167), serene but vacant. Then the images gain in turbulence, become stormy seas, and reminiscences of the city return, now ironically invested with a setting of triumphant chaos:

Hitherto the human face had mixed often in my dreams, but not despotically, nor with any special power of tormenting. But now that which I have called the tyranny of the human face began to unfold itself. Perhaps some part of my London life might be answerable for this. Be that as it may, now it was that upon the rocking waters of the ocean the human face began to appear: the sea appeared paved with innumerable faces, upturned to the heavens: faces, imploring, wrathful, despairing, surged upwards by thousands, by myriads, by generations, by centuries: – my agitation was infinite, – my mind tossed – and surged with the ocean.   (C 167)

The process of dissolution is complete. The great, aspiring clouds of the early visions have descended into the infinite ocean of despair, the towers of the celestial city have yielded before the modern urban aggregate of the human swarm, the myriad faces that conceal the lost face of love for which the dreamer is ultimately seeking. Unable to control surging energies, he is at last tossed about on their surfaces. By arranging this sequence of dreams to start with the transcendent synthesis and to end with its disintegrated form in the jumbled components of experience De Quincey implicitly presents a parable of the imagination's incapacity to retain the vision of splendour.

The second sequence of dreams retains throughout its course the intensity of terror in which the first has ended, but in a complementary opposite form. The oceanic chaos now coalesces again, and the menaces of the indefinite turn into active agents of persecution. The paranoid nightmares that constitute the second set of dreams ironically restore that sense of imminent divinity, of relation between subject and object, of the dreamer at the centre of his cosmos, which the Piranesi vision of existential reality denies. The disjunctive emblems of a nameless horror not only begin to acquire a vast personified power in De Quincey's imagination but also to attract his fascination. He broods on 'the ancient, monumental, cruel, and elaborate religions of Indostan' (C 168), and his dreams are filled with a hysterical assortment of Asiatic religious persecutions:

I ran into pagodas: and was fixed, for centuries, at the summit, or in secret rooms; I was the idol; I was the priest; I was worshipped; I was sacrificed. I fled from the wrath of Brama through all the forests of Asia: Vishnu hated me: Seeva laid wait for me. I came suddenly upon Isis and Osiris: I had done a deed, they said, which the ibis and the crocodile trembled at. I was buried, for a thousand years, in stone coffins, with mummies and sphinxes, in narrow chambers at the heart of eternal pyramids. I was kissed, with cancerous kisses, by crocodiles; and laid, confounded with all unutterable slimy things, amongst reeds and Nilotic mud.   (C 170)

Religious awe, once located in a portrait of maternal benevolence at school, now invests forms that are unutterably alien and bizarre; a milieu of interrelated concern, once epitomized by the various acts of generosity which De Quincey received in his early adventures, is re-created here in the strange gods' obsessive concern with his deeds; reciprocity and a sense of exchanged divinity, once present in his relation with Ann, now recur in his alternation in the roles of idol, devotee, and victim. These monstrous parodies of the idea of spiritual community suggest an imagination *in extremis*, one forced to substitute dire impingements and a community of horror in place of a reality that has become void of significant forms.

At this point the dream-sequence has attained a character which the typical state of Coleridgean dejection no longer represents adequately and which is more closely related to the night-worlds of later romanticism, the perverse attractions to horror found in Poe, in Beddoes, and in certain of the *symbolistes* in France. This perverse attraction is evident here in the relation of the dreamer to the crocodile, a parody of exchanged love. Not only does the crocodile offer the dreamer 'cancerous kisses,' but as its visage multiplies into 'a thousand repetitions,' the dreamer stands 'loathing and fascinated' (c 172). Their relationship becomes permanent: 'The cursed crocodile became to me the object of more horror than almost all the rest. I was compelled to live with him; and (as was always the case almost in my dreams) for centuries' (c 171–2). These suggestions of a perverse love-affair are perhaps only half ironic. The helpless fascination, the powerlessness to resist hint at a luxuriation in despair beneath the conscious loathing, a prostration to imagined horrors so complete that only the notion of long centuries of submission to affectionate reptilian assaults can render it accurately.

As if the vein of horror has temporarily exhausted itself, a kind of adagio ensues in the third sequence of dreams, in which De Quincey returns to the theme of experiential loss and imaginative hope. In this sequence the dreamer does not attempt to scale celestial heights, but to enter the domain of the dream-pastoral, where one may gain solace by merging loss into beauty. These dreams open, appropriately for their theme, on Easter Sunday, and their physical setting represents an amalgam of Grasmere and Jerusalem, of rugged mountains and placid lawns, of burgeoning roses and verdant graves (c 174–5). Here the natural beauties of this world and the Christian portents of the next seek to transfigure that vacant centre of death which lies between them. It is in this centre that De Quincey discovers Ann, sitting like a Magdalene among the Judaean palms:

She fixed her eyes upon me earnestly; and I said to her at length: 'So then I have found you at last.' I waited: but she answered me not a word. Her face was the same as when I saw it last, and yet again how different! ... She seemed more beautiful than she was at that time, but in all other points the same, and not older. Her looks were tranquil, but with unusual solemnity of expression; and I now gazed upon her with some awe.   (c 176–7)

Ann's disappearance from the experiential world of Oxford Street has enabled her to occupy in De Quincey's imagination the position of an attendant at the threshold of harmonies that transcend the experiential altogether. But again the vital faith is missing, for no risen redeemer appears to lead the seeker beyond the threshold. The dreamer has sought to recapture a love that flowered in adverse experience, and the Ann who dwells in this dream-setting can answer nothing that would satisfy such a quest. As she retains her unearthly silence, her face altered and yet not altered, like that of a corpse, there arises the uneasy quality of an interview between a living mortal and a shade in the underworld. The portents of resurrection, both natural and spiritual, thus remain sterile, and that centre of death which they were supposed to transfigure spreads its silence over the whole scene, turning beauty into funereal effects.

De Quincey thus fails in his attempt to recover Ann by investing her memory with the special effects of the dream-pastoral, and the vision consequently crumbles into the naked memory of experience which was its foundation: 'I perceived vapours rolling between us; in a moment, all had vanished; thick darkness came on; and, in the twinkling of an eye, I was far away from mountains, and by lamp-light in Oxford street, walking again with Ann – just as we walked seventeen years before, when we were both children' (C 177). With the trappings of the dream-pastoral gone the imagination restores the essential form of De Quincey's desires, the recovery of a remembered innocence. But this restoration offers only what he has already possessed in memory, and if its imagery contains more tangible vitality than that present in the dream-pastoral, mere waking shall cause the loss once more of what has already been lost in experience.

All of the motifs of 'The Pains of Opium' appear assembled, explicitly or implicitly, in a kind of apocalyptic finale that puts the seal of irrevocability on De Quincey's separation from love. Unlike the earlier vision of the celestial city, this final dream picks up a different strand of apocalyptic imagery, that of the confrontation of ultimate powers, the moment of awful battle:

The dream commenced with a music which now I often heard in dreams – a music of preparation and of awakening suspense; a music like the opening of the Coronation Anthem, and which, like *that*, gave the feeling of a vast march – of infinite cavalcades filing off – and the tread of innumerable armies. The morning was come of a mighty day – a day of crisis and of final hope for human nature, then suffering some mysterious eclipse, and labouring in some dread extremity ... Some greater interest was at stake; some mightier cause than ever yet the sword had pleaded, or trumpet proclaimed. (C 178)

De Quincey depicts here the preparation for a battle like Armageddon, that point where the forces of good and evil have become wholly polarized so that decisive battle may be joined. Obviously he has retained the personification of evil acquired in the visions of persecution, and he imagines all of humanity under its sway, 'labouring in some dread extremity.' Instead of bringing a final deliverance, however, the apocalyptic forces induce in the dreamer an increasing bewilderment, and what is worse, just at that point when it becomes apparent that he must master these forces if the victory is to ensue:

Somewhere, I knew not where – somehow, I knew not how – by some beings, I knew not whom – a battle, a strife, an agony, was conducting, – was evolving like a great drama, or piece of music; with which my sympathy was the more insupportable from my confusion as to its place, its cause, its nature, and its possible issue. I, as is usual in dreams (where, of necessity, we make ourselves central to every movement), had the power, and yet had not the power, to decide it. I had the power, if I could raise myself, to will it; and yet again had not the power, for the weight of twenty Atlantics was upon me, or the oppression of inexpiable guilt. (c 178)

He is incapable of willing the victory into being, because he cannot master its operative forces, and this because he has lost faith in his power of supplying vital connections. His imagination, which in an earlier vision 'tossed and surged' on an ocean of formlessness, has now sunk deep within it. It is implicitly a surrender, and it creates a burden of guilt that is inexpiable because it is welded to inertia in a grim circularity of cause and effect. In its external reference this dream is perhaps a recapitulation of De Quincey's failure to complete *De emendatione humani intellectus*, that work of philosophic synthesis which was to have contributed to 'the exaltation of human nature,' but its inward reference is probably to the war between his imaginative power and his despair. In the embrace of this monster of the deep he witnesses the defeat of the forces of light and hears the victorious powers proclaim the irrevocable severance from all the forms that he has loved:

... darkness and lights: tempest and human faces: and at last, with the sense that all was lost, female forms, and the features that were worth all the world to me, and but a moment allowed, – and clasped hands, and heart-breaking partings, and then – everlasting farewells! And with a sigh, such as the caves of hell sighed when the incestuous mother uttered the abhorred name of death, the sound was reverberated – everlasting farewells! and again, and yet again reverberated – everlasting farewells!
     And I awoke in struggles, and cried aloud – 'I will sleep no more!' (c 179)

In echoing with this final cry Macbeth's self-aimed prophecy of damnation De Quincey may be affirming the indelibility of his guilt, the incurable maiming of his imagination. But the cry is really more equivocal, for the region of sleep was the site of his nightmares, and the few pages that remain in the work, describing his successful efforts to decrease his consumption of opium, present the ordeal in terms of a passage to rebirth in a better state: 'it may be as painful to be born as to die: I think it probable: and, during the whole period of diminishing the opium, I had the torments of a man passing out of one mode of existence into another. The issue was not death, but a sort of physical regeneration' (C 184). But the precise nature of this state of wakeful regeneration remains obscure as does the source of his strength of will to fight the drug, a strength presumed to be unavailable in the visions themselves. The work thus draws to a close on a note of expectant indeterminacy, a sense of unquestionable loss that brings with it a not readily specified gain. This sense is clearly conveyed in the fine paragraph which concludes the book:

One memorial of my former condition still remains: my dreams are not yet perfectly calm: the dread swell and agitation of the storm have not wholly subsided: the legions that encamped in them are drawing off, but not all departed: my sleep is still tumultuous, and, like the gates of Paradise to our first parents when looking back from afar, it is still (in the tremendous line of Milton) –
    With dreadful faces throng'd and fiery arms. (C 184–5)

Once again the literary analogue is of equivocal import. In one sense it captures (and aggrandizes) De Quincey's retrospective mood as he looks back upon the sum of his imaginative experience, the domain of ultimate desires crowded with the prohibitory figures of nemesis. The 'dreadful faces' of De Quincey's experience, however, are demonic usurpers rather than angelic guardians and the distanced vantage-point from which he observes them promises renewed possibilities more than it confirms the extent of his fall.

  Such ambiguity of mood is not of course absent from the Miltonic passage from which he draws his quotation, as its full context shows:

        They looking back, all th' Eastern side beheld
        Of Paradise, so late their happie seat,
        Wav'd over by that flaming Brand, the Gate
        With dreadful Faces throngd and fierie Armes:
        Som natural tears they dropd, but wip'd them soon;
        The World was all before them, where to choose
        Thir place of rest, and Providence thir guide.[8]

The sense of redeeming compensation implicit in the last three lines of this passage allowed Wordsworth, we recall from the beginning of this chapter, to employ the penultimate line as a starting-point for an epic of spiritual adventures independent of orthodox sanctions. De Quincey's own autobiographical account ultimately confronts the same passage from *Paradise Lost* where Wordsworth finds his beginning, although in the *Confessions* quotation once again stops just short of those lines that give the passage an optimistic context. In this later work of Romantic subjectivity there is a kind of return to the Miltonic sense of a paradise indeed lost.

The *Confessions* must end tentatively, for it has offered two contradictory alternatives, the expansion and the contraction of the individual soul, as consequences of an experiental loss, and it wholly repudiates neither of them. De Quincey's uncertainty as to the true nature of his experience probably contributes in large part to the pervasive obliquity of utterance, that manipulation of façades, discussed earlier in this chapter. By resolving the warfare within his imagination into the play of symptoms connected with a crisis of addiction, undoubtedly accurate in its rendering, he gives a determinacy of form to the book which the deepest impulses involved in its writing do not possess. But thematic indeterminacy and obliquity are not necessarily detriments at this stage in the writer's creative life, whatever special methods of exegesis they demand from the critic. The world is all before De Quincey too, although its materials are of his own making, the symbols and motifs that compose the *Confessions*. Although I propose to describe in the following chapters a chronological arc of imaginative development in De Quincey's career, it is proper to note that he is essentially one of those writers whose successive works refine a fundamental vision rather than alter it. Like a cartographer remapping a certain territory or portions of it in varying scales, he sometimes offers clarifying synopses of the whole vision, sometimes detailed enlargements of a part. The variety and indeed the development of his work come from his sense of never feeling quite sure which map is the *right* map, the truly adequate one. Out of the adumbrations of the *Confessions* come a series of minor sketches in the next two decades, efforts directed towards that unachieved sufficiency. These works show in new forms the imaginative preoccupation with isolation and power that have marked the self portrayed here, now deeply immersed in the vicissitudes of experience.

❧[3]❧

Modes of Power:
Speculations and Fictions, 1823-1838

Not until the publication of *Suspiria de Profundis* in 1845 does there appear among De Quincey's writings a work similar in scope and intensity to the *Confessions* of 1821-2. Copious journalistic activity fills the intervening period, much of the work undistinguished yet occasionally flaring with an imaginative power that reminds us of his creative strength at its best. The biographical reasons for this long submergence of inward and visionary concerns are not germane to this study, though one can readily imagine how a combination of domestic and financial exigencies could force a writer away from topics which demand leisure for meditation and slow stylistic elaboration. More to the point in an account of De Quincey's imaginative development, the very achievement of the *Confessions* becomes something of an obstacle to the expression of that mixture of reflection, introspective delving, and visionary narrative which is his forte. At once self-revelatory and diffident, the *Confessions* makes another major autobiographical work impossible for a number of years. Thus further explorations of imaginative concerns, tentatively broached in the *Confessions*, tend to occur in masked forms in short stories, novels, and occasional essays, or in sudden bursts of rhetoric, rich with metaphoric resonance, appearing in the midst of unimaginative prose. If opium-eating in the earlier work serves as an excuse for presenting alternative visions of the self polarized in extremes of apotheosis and damnation, the imaginative works that immediately follow treat the same polarization externally in terms of legendary figures, heroes and murderers, great artists and demons, helpless victims and threatening cosmic powers.

All these figures play a role in De Quincey's imaginative meditation upon a power whose effects seem omnipresent although its locus is constantly shifting, now housed in transcendent figures called God or Satan or Death, now within the subjective imagination or alternatively within the congregated might of experiential forces. Like Shelley, De Quincey is obsessed with power as an awful unseen presence that will not speak its name, although he lacks Shelley's humanistic faith in its beneficent efficacy. Every one of De Quincey's imaginative works attempts in some degree or other to track this power through its various transformations, and the attempt seems to be the major imaginative enterprise of the middle period of his career. Although his phrase 'the literature of power' is famous, it has often seemed merely a synonym for imaginative as opposed to discursive writing. But De Quincey's own practice gives the phrase new connotations, suggesting as it does a literature that is about *power* as a dominating subject, a literature that seeks to approach it, define it, and eventually subdue it to the author's own aesthetic purposes and ambitions.

De Quincey's first discussion of the literature of power occurs in the middle of 'Letters to a Young Man Whose Education Has Been Neglected' (x, 9–80), one of the various journalistic pieces which he produced for the *London Magazine* in 1823. On the whole, it is a rather fustian assemblage of its author's crotchets concerning education and scholarship, its title suggesting a sad scaling-down of the unwritten *De emendatione humani intellectus* that was the focus of De Quincey's earlier philosophic ambitions. Yet abruptly in the midst of these modest 'Letters' he expresses an ambition for literature rivalling that of philosophy on its highest plane, and the manner of this expression, impassioned and full of imaginative resonance, is such as to make the discussion a miniature exemplum of what it describes:

All that is literature seeks to communicate power; all that is not literature, to communicate knowledge. Now, if it be asked what is meant by communicating power, I, in my turn, would ask by what name a man would designate the case in which I should be made to feel vividly, and with a vital consciousness, emotions which ordinary life rarely or never supplies occasions for exciting, and which had previously lain unwakened, and hardly within the dawn of consciousness – as myriads of modes of feeling are at this moment in every human mind for want of a poet to organize them? I say, when these inert and sleeping forms *are* organized, when these possibilities *are* actualized, is this conscious and living possession of mine *power*, or what is it?

When, in King Lear, the height, and depth, and breadth, of human passion is revealed to us, and, for the purposes of a sublime antagonism, is revealed in the weakness of an old man's nature, and in one night two worlds of storm are brought face to face – the human world, and the world of physical nature – mirrors of each other, semichoral antiphonies, strophe and anti-strophe heaving with rival convulsions, and with the double darkness of night and madness, – when I am thus suddenly startled into a feeling of the infinity of the world within me, is this power, or what may I call it? Space, again, what is it in most men's minds? The lifeless form of the world without us, a postulate of the geometrician, with no more vitality or real existence to their feelings than the square root of two. But, if Milton has been able to *inform* this empty theatre, peopling it with Titanic shadows, forms that sat at the eldest counsels of the infant world, chaos and original night, –

'Ghostly shapes,
To meet at noontide, Fear and trembling Hope,
Death the Skeleton,
And Time the Shadow,' –

so that, from being a thing to inscribe with diagrams, it has become under his hands a vital agent on the human mind, – I presume that I may justly express the tendency of the Paradise Lost by saying that it communicates power; a pretension far above all communication of knowledge.   (x, 48–9)

As a description of a formal theory of literature this is virtually useless, and critics such as René Wellek are right to complain of the 'vagueness and multiplicity of meanings' in the term 'power' (in this passage it variously signifies material cause, agency, and effect).[1] Yet it is precisely this elusiveness at the centre that gives the passage its imaginative force, and De Quincey himself appears to stress the elusiveness of power by approaching the term with circumspection ('is this conscious and living possession of mine *power*, or what is it?'; 'is this power, or what may I call it?'). The rhetorical questions attempt to persuade us that power is a real substance underlying the literary phenomena described, something discovered and not merely a heuristic term, but at the same time they suggest an uneasiness about coming too close to any actual analysis of that substance. Any attempt to push the question further, to insist on a definition of the nature of this power, sends us back to the web of metaphors which De Quincey has woven about his literary instances from Shakespeare and Milton. This proves a fruitful direction to take, for these metaphors, though adding little to the strength of the passage as a propositional statement, allow us to view it as an imaginative argument more significant to an understanding of De Quincey's work than any discursive proposition could be.

Of the two paragraphs quoted above, the first concerns power as a 'conscious living possession' of the individual reader, a subjective awakening to vitality, whereas the second concerns power as something contained within and reverberating out of the literary works themselves. These subjective and objective forms of power are described by radically different sets of metaphors. The ideas of the first paragraph are firmly grounded in Wordsworthian and Coleridgean conceptions of the function of poetry as an act of realizing the latent organic unity of the self, a self thereby renewed and exalted, and hence the appropriateness of the images of sleeping and awakening, inertness and vitality.[2] When De Quincey turns to describing the power inherent in *Lear* and *Paradise Lost*, the organic metaphors of the first paragraph drop out, and the world of Shakespeare and Milton emerges not as a universe of vital utterance but as a vast cosmic space. Thus human passion has 'height, and depth, and breadth,' 'two worlds' are 'brought face to face,' an 'infinity ... within' is evoked, and Euclidean space is transformed into mythic space, the abode of 'chaos and original night.' These spatial images are made dynamic through apparent doublings, multiplications, and self-projections. The 'two worlds of storm' are 'mirrors' of each other, a doubling that is redoubled when the forms externally present on Shakespeare's page are projected and reduplicated as the 'infinity of the world within.' Just as Shakespeare projects worlds upon the space within, Milton projects 'Titanic shadows,' as in a lantern show, upon our empirical notion of the space without. This space, called an 'empty theatre,' suggests the theatrical nature of the whole complex of metaphors here described, a suggestion enforced by the references to 'semichoral antiphonies, strophe and antistrophe.'

Despite De Quincey's talk of vital consciousness as a description of the power when it dwells within, from his metaphoric evocation of its external dwelling-place in this vast theatre it seems clear that the drama it produces has nothing to do with human concerns. Lear confronts in agony the moral condition of mankind, Satan moves through the void to corrupt the innocent order of Eden, and De Quincey can see only a kind of *symphonie lumière*, a multiplication of 'worlds,' projections of shadows, fearful symmetries of images in various poised and dynamic relations with one another. Shakespeare and Milton become in this vision not makers of human meaning but representatives of the self-withdrawn Demi-urge, the tokens of whose power remain in electrical kindlings and glimpses of the abyss afforded to the reader-spectator. The alternative modes of power seem antipathetic, assuming the forms of a dazzling yet certainly terrifying cosmos and a warm, vital self which the other mode of power must somehow awaken.

This problem in the passage on the 'literature of power' provides a paradigm of the problem that is to dominate De Quincey's imaginative writings, minor and major, a problem first suggested in the equivocal alternatives of the pleasures and pains of opium in the *Confessions*. Power leaps unpredictably from cosmos to self or the other way round, sometimes assuming overwhelming forms from without, sometimes flowing from within as a benign gift of self-possession and control over one's environment. In the discussion of the literature of power De Quincey gives us an impression of the goal to which the working of the literary imagination (that of the reader as well as the author) should tend, but he does not explain how it happens. The indeterminacy of this passage makes sense only if we think of it in terms of an implicit quest. Thus the vast theatre of cosmic power must by its vastness hold out a conspicuous invitation for the self to fill it; as self-consciousness expands, the theatre shrinks until the outer shows of dynamic forms are all inside the self and have become the inner fountains of a personal vitality. In this way the power of the imagined becomes the power of imagining, the power of creating the universe in which one lives. The 'young man' whom De Quincey addresses is invited to make his own quest for the appropriation of power, but the achievement which his tutor seems here to have reached at least in his experience of sublime literature is not so easily gained in the actual making of a literature of power. De Quincey's bewilderment at the various permutations of power continues in later and more narrowly focused writings on the subject, and we do well at this point to move from paradigm to instance, starting with another work of 1823 signally important to his literary reputation.

II DEMONIC POWER: TWO ESSAYS ON MURDER

De Quincey's preoccupation with Shakespeare as a poet of power continues in the justly famous 'On the Knocking at the Gate in *Macbeth*,' which provides a brilliant illustration of the generalized comments on poetic power contained in the 'Letters to a Young Man' written a few months before. The *Macbeth* essay is properly valued as De Quincey's most acute study of the relation in a work of art of specific incident to basic affective pattern, but, like the comments on 'the literature of power,' it invites us into his own imaginative world as much as it illuminates the subject of his criticism. Beyond its immediate concern with a particular scene in a particular play the essay aims to provide further documentation for the validity of Shakespeare's Romantic apotheosis as a poet gifted with the multitudinousness of nature and the designing powers of God:

O mighty poet! Thy works are not as those of other men, simply and merely great works of art, but are also like the phenomena of nature, like the sun and the sea, the stars and the flowers, like frost and snow, rain and dew, hail-storm and thunder, which are to be studied with entire submission of our own faculties, and in the perfect faith that in them there can be not too much or too little, nothing useless or inert, but that, the farther we press in our discoveries, the more we shall see proofs of design and self-supporting arrangement where the careless eye had seen nothing but accident! (x, 393–4)

The occasion for this culminating apostrophe derives from De Quincey's long-standing perplexity about the knocking at the gate of Macbeth's castle after the murder of Duncan. The incident is apparently trivial, its presence in the play even arbitrary, yet for De Quincey it has always seemed to endow the murderer with 'peculiar awfulness and a depth of solemnity' (x, 389). Evidently we have here a test-case of the problematic relation between accident and design. The knocking at the gate in itself seems to belong to the world of accident, the succession of arbitrary and random experiences apparently swept up by the all-encompassing dramatist in his desire to depict the small as well as the grand events of his world; yet that 'peculiar awfulness' attendant on the incident argues for the presence of a controlling design which makes its effects known through phenomena but conceals its mode of operation. In trying to unveil that mode De Quincey's essay becomes another in a series of quests for the locus and nature of a more than ordinary power.

The essay as a whole is striking for the peculiar aristocracy of its tone. Its conclusion, quoted above, not only sets apart Shakespeare's works from those of all other men, but also makes a distinction between the 'careless eye,' which sees only accident in life, and the eye schooled deeply in intuitive receptiveness, which sees design. Early in the essay, in a somewhat digressive paragraph, De Quincey presents an analogous distinction regarding skill in drawing. Here the 'careless eye' belongs to the ordinary man, whom the essayist chooses to call an 'idiot,' a man whose 'common-sense' understanding of the real size of objects makes him incapable of drawing things in perspective; at the opposite pole there is the skilled draughtsman, who succeeds by abjuring common sense and relying on his 'intuitive knowledge of the laws of vision' (x, 390). These distinctions seem harmless enough, but the ensuing discussion of the famous murderer John Williams (recalled because one of his crimes also involved a door-knocking incident) reveals the perverse potential of such distinctions of superiority and inferiority. De Quincey speaks (anticipating the tone of his later 'Murder Considered as One of the Fine Arts') of Williams's 'unparalleled murders which have procured for him such a brilliant and undying reputation ... All other murders look pale by the deep crimson of his' (x, 390). Such language clearly parodies in advance the terms which are to be applied to Shakespeare himself at the end of the paper. De Quincey's own unstated sense of aristocratic superiority over the 'common-sense' understanding clearly emerges in the witty artfulness with which he coalesces – in a figure such as Williams – associations derived from Shakespeare's subject-matter in *Macbeth* and associations derived from his stature as a poet.

Playfulness in De Quincey's prose often serves to cushion the potentially disturbing effects of recognizing the nature of his serious concerns, although this nature becomes clear enough when he finally devotes his attention to an analysis of Shakespeare's artistic motives in *Macbeth*:

Murder, in ordinary cases, where the sympathy is wholly directed to the case of the murdered person, is an incident of coarse and vulgar horror; and for this reason, – that it flings the interest exclusively upon the natural but ignoble instinct by which we cleave to life: an instinct which, as being indispensable to the primal law of self-preservation, is the same in kind (though different in degree) amongst all living creatures. This instinct, therefore, because it annihilates all distinctions, and degrades the greatest of men to the level of 'the poor beetle that we tread on,' exhibits human nature in its most abject and humiliating attitude. Such an attitude would little suit the purposes of the poet. What must he then do? He must throw the interest on the murderer. (x, 391)

The aristocratic distinctions are, then, more disturbing than one could previously have suspected. It is not merely a matter of great artists, or great murderers, and inferior practitioners; clearly the murderer is also the aristocratic superior of the murdered. It is curious to observe how the natural instinct for self-preservation becomes 'ignoble,' a general leveller, to which the poet would never ally himself, especially if an unnatural (and therefore noble?) murderer is at hand.

If the 'natural' maintenance of life is ignoble, then the murderer who chooses to destroy life at will surpasses nature and enters the world of design through his exercise of Titanic will.[3] Thus De Quincey's Macbeth becomes a Miltonic villain, a reflex of the subjective creativity translated to the demonic mode: 'But in the murderer, such a murderer as a poet will condescend to, there must be raging some great storm of passion – jealousy, ambition, vengeance, hatred – which will create a hell within him, and into this hell we are to look' (x, 392). It is here that De Quincey broaches the centre of his argument: a Satanic Macbeth must have a hell to operate in, a world free from the ignoble routine of ordinary phenomena, and such a hell, to conform to its traditional archetype, must have a gate. The cadenza of prose which expresses this argument is one of the finest passages in De Quincey's works, the kind of sudden visionary conception that organizes all that surrounds it into the tissue of imaginative art:

All action in any direction is best expounded, measured, and made apprehensible, by reaction. Now, apply this to the case in *Macbeth*. Here, as I have said, the retiring of the human heart and the entrance of the fiendish heart was to be expressed and made sensible. Another world has stept in; and the murderers are taken out of the region of human things, human purposes, human desires. They are transfigured: Lady Macbeth is 'unsexed'; Macbeth has forgot that he was born of woman; both are conformed to the image of devils; and the world of devils is suddenly revealed. But how shall this be conveyed and made palpable? In order that a new world may step in, this world must for a time disappear. The murderers and the murder must be insulated – cut off by an immeasurable gulf from the ordinary tide and succession of human affairs – locked up and sequestered in some deep recess; we must be made sensible that the world of ordinary life is suddenly arrested, laid asleep, tranced, racked into a dread armistice; time must be annihilated, relation to things without abolished; and all must pass self-withdrawn into a deep syncope and suspension of earthly passion. Hence it is that, when the deed is done, when the work of darkness is perfect, then the world of darkness passes away like a pageantry in the clouds: the knocking at the gate is heard, and it makes known audibly that the reaction has commenced; the human has made its reflux upon the fiendish; the pulses of life are beginning to beat again; and the re-establishment of the goings-on of the world in which we live first makes us profoundly sensible of the awful parenthesis that had suspended them. (x, 393)

The tendency towards hierarchical differentiation already observed in the essay acquires here a new dimension of meaning, for it is no longer a distinction of worth but one of modes of being. Just as Lear and his heath become 'two worlds of storm' in De Quincey's description of the literature of power, here too Macduff knocking at the gate is transformed into 'the world of ordinary life,' 'the world in which we live,' and the castle of Inverness into 'the world of darkness.' De Quincey's quest for the power of Shakespeare's art leads him to the threshold of a 'deep recess' of uncontingent being beyond time, beyond 'earthly passion.' If the murderer's ruthless power of will brings this world of darkness into being, it is the state itself and not the deed that holds De Quincey's deepest fascination, a state considered demonic not because of any moral principle but because of the terrifying play of absolute freedom that it affords.

The lacuna in ordinary time in which the deed occurs is filled with a kind of 'dream-time,' to use Georges Poulet's phrase,[4] for the powerful effect of the knocking at the gate, as De Quincey describes it, is precisely equivalent to the power that vivid dreams hold over our waking experience. This is not merely because the language of the passage intimates a dream-like state ('the world of ordinary life is suddenly arrested, laid asleep, tranced, racked into dread armistice') but, more significantly, because De Quincey locates our recognition of the atemporal world's existence precisely at the point of its temporal abolition, when Macduff's knocking reintroduces the world of ordinary life. The pattern for this insight may be found in the most familiar example of discontinuity of consciousness in our everyday lives, the awakening from a dream, for the moment of the dream's vanishing is also the moment of awareness of the dream *as* dream, awareness (sometimes terrifying) of unknown modes of consciousness at work beneath the level of ordinary understanding. The spatial and temporal focal points of this crucial episode in the play, a gate and a moment of knocking, thus correspond to the point when the spectator realizes that he has just experienced not a sequence of events in ordinary time but a vision of atemporal being. It is as if the murderous events at the centre of *Macbeth* become our dream, the knocking at the gate forming the point where accident becomes design (for the canny interpreter of dreams and dream-like art), and commonplace understanding becomes intuition.

It must be clear by now how far De Quincey's sneers at the ordinary man and his suggestive linkings of murderer, artist, and intuitive spectator are from any real adoption of a sardonic *ésthetique du mal* (although his supplementary considerations in 'Murder Considered as One of the

Fine Arts' were influential in the trend towards Decadence). De
Quincey's Shakespeare is essentially a master of a gate between worlds, a
conductor into a darkness beyond life where the envisioned murderer
and the spectator dwell together. The playwright becomes somewhat like
the 'celestial druggist' of the opium-eater's confessions, providing the
agency for displacing acts that are squalid and repulsive in the everyday
realm from out of that realm, so that they become the content for a fantasy of unfettered will. We should be quick to observe that the two dominating fantasy figures of the manifestly self-referent *Confessions*, power
as 'majestic intellect' and power as demonic threat, not only reappear
here in alternative forms of 'mighty poet' and murderer but are much
more overtly identified. As an essay exploring recessive states of consciousness, 'The Knocking at the Gate' also displays De Quinceyan
manoeuvres that we can now take to be characteristic when he tries to
deal with matters related to his anxieties and desires. The essay manages
to express and conceal, recoil from and yet admire, power in its alternating
and coalescing disguises of destruction and art. This cagey elusiveness,
precipitating as it does the expansive flow of language that reveals a vision
of the atemporal world, marks De Quincey himself as a Janus-figure at the
gate with its advantageous perspectives upon equivocal selves.

De Quincey's first paper on 'Murder Considered as One of the Fine Arts,'
published in *Blackwood's Magazine* in 1827, represents a bizarre expansion upon those brief phrases in the *Macbeth* essay referring to John
Williams's 'unparalleled murders' and his 'brilliant and undying reputation.' Williams returns at the start of the new essay as one who 'has
exalted the ideal of murder to all of us' (XIII, 12), one who now finds a
literary peer not in Shakespeare but in Wordsworth, for the murderer
too 'has in a manner "created the taste by which he is to be enjoyed"'
(XIII, 12). Other blandly brazen misappropriations of common aesthetic
dicta crop up elsewhere in the essay: for example, murder considered
artistically serves 'to humanize the heart' (XIII, 48) and fosters the same
purpose 'as that of tragedy in Aristotle's account of it; viz. "to cleanse the
heart by means of pity and terror"' (XIII, 47), so that the piece takes on
the appearance of a parody of aesthetic theorizing. The appearance is
misleading, however, for what 'Murder as One of the Fine Arts' scrupu-
lously avoids throughout is any systematic parallel of the burlesqued
model such as gives true parody its identifying form. Not only does De
Quincey generally avert his glance from any serious aesthetic doctrines
but he also studiously keeps at bay any intruding visions of horrifying

violence such as have attracted his fascination in the essay on *Macbeth*.[5] No acts of murder are actually described in the paper of 1827 (only in the famous 'Postscript' of 1854 does De Quincey actually confront Williams's crimes). The mask of connoisseur of murder pretends to hide the work of the parodist, but this also turns out to be a mask, for the real substance of the essay is an exercise in elusiveness.

In form the paper of 1827 rambles from anecdote to anecdote, always wittily, yet the wit largely derives from the distance that any given anecdote can travel away from its ostensible subject-matter while appearing to entertain it. For example, a sizable portion of the essay is devoted to arguing, with about as much seriousness as the case warrants, that all the great philosophers from Descartes to Kant were either murdered, almost murdered, or subject to the threat of murder. One representative passage is a good sample of the mode of De Quincey's *jeu d'esprit*:

As Leibnitz, though not murdered, may be said to have died partly of the fear that he should be murdered, and partly out of vexation that he was not, Kant, on the other hand – had a narrower escape from a murderer than any man we read of except Des Cartes ... For health's sake, Kant imposed upon himself, at one time, a walk of six miles every day along a high road. This fact becoming known to a man who had his private reasons for commiting murder, at the third milestone from Königsberg he waited for his 'intended,' who came up to time as duly as a mail-coach. But for an accident, Kant was a dead man. This accident lay in the scrupulous, or what Mrs. Quickly would have called the *peevish* morality of the murderer. An old professor, he fancied might be laden with sins. Not so a young child. On this consideration, he turned away from Kant at the critical moment, and soon after murdered a child of five years old. Such is the German account of the matter; but my opinion is that the murderer was an amateur, who felt how little would be gained to the cause of good taste by murdering an arid, and adust metaphysician: there was no room for display, as the man could not possibly look more like a mummy when dead than he had done alive.   (XIII, 34–5)

Such a passage gives us a topsyturvy world, where homicide is inevitable but unmotivated, where conscience is considered a lucky accident, where 'scrupulous morality' leads to the murdering of a child, and metaphysicians are identified with mummies. What keeps all these inversions and deflations of conventional notions from affecting us with their potential morbidity is the dead-pan aplomb of the skilled raconteur who skips lightly away from nonsense stated as if it were established fact, pauses

pregnantly in order to surprise us more effectively with further absurdi-
ties, and thereby turns all his remarks into jokes. Indeed the whole paragraph is arranged like a long and elaborate joke which culminates in a
sudden descent of emphasis on an unexpected source of humor, in this
case, Kant's ludicrous appearance. That the joke should finally centre on
Kant rather than on murder illustrates De Quincey's skill in diverting
his reader from the macabre theme that is his stated subject-matter while
using that theme as the energizing agent for a succession of comic inversions.

By locating destructive power in a topsyturvy nonsense world the
raconteur achieves the same dislocation of a real-life threat into a world
of fantasy that the intuitive quasi-dreamer of the *Macbeth* essay accom-
plishes in the demonic mode. It is easy to surmise that the covert aim of
'Murder as One of the Fine Arts' is a dissipation of impinging threat, and
such a surmise need not look for support from De Quincey's more obvious manifestations of anxiety elsewhere. The very attempt within the
essay itself to conceal the dissipating technique provides its own evidence. Hence the primary mask of the perverse connoisseur of homicide
endows the narrator with the attributes of a privileged figure of power
himself, while the secondary mask of pseudo-parodist ensures another
kind of privileged security, that of the moral satirist. The trouble with
such devices is that they cannot sustain themselves indefinitely with
success. Either the horror will break out openly or the devices will
become tedious, too obviously a shoddy and flimsy covering for the real
obsessions. The real horror of murder finally emerges in the 'Postscript'
of 1854, but the second paper on 'Murder as One of the Fine Arts,' published in 1839, tries only to prolong the fun of the first. This fictitious
account of a banquet of the Society of Connoisseurs in Murder is pervasively uninspired in its attempt to recreate the former *jeu d'esprit*. It is
noteworthy for only one remarkable passage in which De Quincey's
whimsical manner attains a virtually eighteenth-century elegance of
expression. Disclaiming any moral approval of murder, his persona goes
on to note that 'if once a man indulges himself in murder, very soon he
comes to think little of robbing, and from robbing he comes next to
drinking and Sabbath-breaking, and from that to incivility and procrastination. Once begin upon this downward path, you never know where
you are to stop' (XIII, 56). This charming inversion of the conventional
moralistic account of the Progress of Vice functions simultaneously as an
evocation of the topsyturvy world of the first paper and as a parody of
complacent moralistic formulations in general. There is also, however, a

peculiar psychological accuracy in the remark. Procrastination, after all, is certainly the most prominent of De Quincey's self-advertised incapacities in the *Confessions* and elsewhere. In the *Confessions* the inward dwelling upon fantasies of personal power or threatened violence have appeared to be intimately connected with the outward incapacity to action, caused by both an excess of will and an excess of fear. It is tempting thus to read this spoofing chain of temporal causation as a not altogether inaccurate rendering of a psychological chain of causation flowing from imagination to outward fact. Behind the procrastinator, the facile and smiling journalist, walks the mighty murderer; behind him, the outlined form of the autonomous imaginative man, an identity too deeply desired to risk its exposure free of disguise.

III GOTHIC TALES: 1823–1838

The themes that move furtively in the essays just considered become more salient in De Quincey's Gothic tales. It is unlikely that these works, some of them merely free translations of German originals, will ever attract many readers, for, as has often been noted, De Quincey's faults as a fiction-writer are glaring – a deaf ear for the rhythms and idioms of actual dialogue and an incapacity for dramatizing sequences of plot (though his powers of suggesting visual spectacle provide substantial if sporadic rewards). Yet De Quincey's natural idiom in fiction is Gothic romance, for no other fictional mode exploits so successfully the sensibility of an imagination that dwells, without the support of divinely instituted value and moral orders, upon the possibilities of enhanced personal power or unmitigated personal threat.[6] We must look beyond the spawn of croaking witches, secret passages, and bloody corpses that infest these Germanic imports into the pages of *Blackwood's* and the *London Magazine* if we wish to understand what, beyond a putative bad taste, attracted De Quincey to them.

The world of demonic power evoked, for example, in 'The Knocking at the Gate' of 1823 finds its fictionalized equivalent in such free translations from the German as 'The Dice' and 'The Fatal Marksman' of the same year, where the demonic presence is Satan himself, whose over-mastering powers are presented as an inexorable and inescapable condition of the hero's existence. In 'The Dice' the hero is foredoomed even before his birth by an ancient prophecy which predicts his traffic with the Evil One, the expected consequences ensuing inevitably; in 'The Fatal Marksman' the hero is trapped into complicity with Satan as the only way of winning his virtuous sweetheart in honourable marriage. If the hero of 'The Dice' is morally corrupted by his complicity with demonic forces, the hero of 'The Fatal Marksman' retains his moral innocence to the end, Satan's powers of ruination operating throughout as an external *deus ex machina*. Tales of damnation virtually without sin such as these display barely a vestige of that crucial moral choice which originally invested the Faust motif with significance. They are more properly kin to dreams and fantasies of an impotent possession and fascination by a total power that defies all canons of order. In allowing the hero, moreover, a temporary omnipotence over circumstance through his complicity with Satanic power, these tales afford a more obvious expression of that momentary participation in the workings of uncontingent power that 'The Knocking at the Gate' hints as occurring for the spectator of the dream-like centre of *Macbeth*.

By ironically counterpointing the hero's temporary omnipotence against the general background of his helplessness avowed adaptations like 'The Fatal Marksman' and 'The Dice' are curiously more expressive of De Quincey's complex imaginings than his own invention *Klosterheim* (published in 1832), a novel in the tradition of Scott's historical romances, where the hero Maximilian glides omnipotently from triumph to triumph in his single-handed defeat of a corrupt and tyrannical government. Even so, Maximilian, however prepossessing, cannot accomplish his designs without undergoing a series of metamorphoses as a student, a general, and finally a mysterious Masque, before he attains his rightful place as the legitimate Prince of Klosterheim. Since Maximilian operates in total privacy, employing secret tunnels that conveniently pierce the city of Klosterheim, the device of masking becomes gratuitous to the workings of the plot and therefore calls attention to itself. De Quincey's attraction to this device of masking here and in several other tales[7] suggests his difficulty in imagining protagonists whose power is inseparable from their day-to-day existence, power uninsulated by roles or changes in state. One recalls how the world of darkness in 'The Knocking at the Gate' must be 'locked up and sequestered in some deep recess' in order to keep its power over the spectator, and how the narrator of 'Murder as One of the Fine Arts' becomes implicitly his own masked hero holding our attention with his nimble feats. The mask of the Gothic protagonist is apparently the reductive equivalent of the displacement devices of narrative artists and the wish-fulfilling transformations of dreamers.

Significantly, when De Quincey eventually creates fictitious protagonists without masks, the whole of ordinary external reality itself suddenly acquires a mask of evil and inescapable power. As the mode of personal power dwindles from the acts of a 'majestic intellect' to an arbitrary talisman of wish-fulfillment, as detachable from the self as a mask, the writer simultaneously suggests its fraudulence and openly proclaims his protagonist's dread of impotence before a universe of potential hostility. This dark concomitant to the flourishing of the self first proclaimed in the *Confessions* openly triumphs in the last and most important of his Gothic fictions, the two novellas of 1838, 'The Household Wreck' and 'The Avenger.' De Quincey's wife Margaret, who appeared briefly in the *Confessions* as a benign tutelary spirit, died in August 1837, and this event may explain his abrupt return to fiction as an outlet for his feelings, six years after the publication of *Klosterheim*. Both tales place at their centre the sufferings of innocent women (the protagonist's wife in 'The Household Wreck,' his mother in 'The Avenger'), hounded to death by the outrages of corrupt and conspiratorial governments, and it is plausible to connect these motifs with the penury and prosecutions for debt which were the De Quincey family's lot during Margaret's final illness.[8] None the less the theme of lost females in De Quincey's writings antedates his wife's death (notably in the treatment of Ann of Oxford Street), so that the theme, whatever its biographical origins, may fitly represent an externalizing of the sense of encirclement by forces of active menace. As a reading of the two novellas shows, anxiety and despair tend to detach themselves from the specific events in the stories which ostensibly generate them and to spread with alarming expansiveness as if seeking to fill every cranny of existence.

Of the two works, 'The Avenger' (published in August 1838) is closer in its spirit and in the devices of its plot to the tales of De Quincey's earlier career. The continuity with the earlier tales manifests itself chiefly in the conventionally Gothic trappings of omnipotence with which the hero is endowed. His name, Max, recalls the hero of *Klosterheim*, and like that incredible figure, he glides effortlessly from house to house with a band of masked followers, committing retributive murders with the kind of inevitability that so often attracts De Quincey's fascination (see XII, 282 ff). In 'The Avenger' De Quincey appears to be still toying with the fantasies of an omnipotent male figure of the sort that interested him in his earlier fictions, and once again the mechanisms of conventional Gothic romance serve the discordant impulses of his imagination well. The career of his avenger-hero shows clearly how fantasies of persecution and impotence can be entertained along with fantasies of power: the son of a wealthy officer during the Napoleonic period and an aristocratic

Jewess, Max witnesses in youth the destruction of his father through French machinations and of his mother and sisters through the anti-Semitism of a narrow-minded German town; he returns to the town in maturity, very rich and handsome, a military hero of melancholy countenance, and loses a second love, Margaret Liebenheim (the name itself suggestive of security and bliss), as an accidental result of his secret career of revenge against the town. It is thus possible to be a pariah and a god, a victim and a destroyer, a sword of justice and an unfettered demon in a single, unswerving career.

These gloomy contraries are of course commonplace attributes of heroes in Gothic fiction, and do not give 'The Avenger' its chief interest. What is striking in the story is an intensity of nihilistic feeling nowhere present in De Quincey's earlier exercises in the Gothic. The opening paragraphs, for example, offer a glimpse into the desperate condition of the imagination itself, a dreaming thing at the centre of a menacing void:

... one feels one's-self sleeping alone, utterly divided from all call or hearing of friends, doors open that should be shut, or unlocked that should be triply secured, the very walls gone, barriers swallowed up by unknown abysses, nothing around one but frail curtains, and a void of illimitable night, whisperings at a distance, correspondence going on between darkness and darkness, like one deep calling to another, and the dreamer's own heart the centre from which the whole network of this unimaginable chaos radiates, by means of which the blank *privations* of silence and darkness become powers the most *positive* and awful. (XII, 236)

In this passage an excess of imagination, bereft on the one hand of external sustenances adequate to its play and on the other hand of limits to its expansion, projects its powers upon vacancy as if they were external forms and then witnesses the knitting together of these forms, now alien powers, as if in a conspiracy to supply the encircling walls of restraint both desired and dreaded. In the context of 'The Avenger' the passage serves as a general reference point for particular perspectives on the threat of baleful external power within the story. De Quincey skilfully varies such perspectives by distributing the burden of narration in part to the hero Max, who tells of the persecutions of his family, and in part to a professor with whom Max lodges during his secret career as an avenger, who describes the acts of vengeance themselves in a narration which frames that of the hero. For Max the 'positive and awful' powers are those of the irrational society that persecuted his mother, the 'tribunal of tyrants all purple and livid with rage' (XII, 277). For the professor the sources of terror are not the deformities of established order but, instead, random and lawless acts of violence, equally irrational, penetrating the otherwise seamless web of ordinary daily life. Each person, it is suggested, is at the centre of his own darkness, which varies its configurations as the position of the beholder varies, though it remains darkness all the same.

The double narration in 'The Avenger' also serves to articulate precisely the division in De Quincey's attitude towards the location of power, by segregating fantasies of personal omnipotence dominating a commonplace external reality from fantasies of personal impotence before an external reality towering up in hostile tyranny. Thus, for example, when the 'I' of the story is the professor, himself a colourless and unremarkable man, whatever possesses power also possesses an uncanny allure as if of a provenance quite beyond the ordinary. He is fascinated with the strangeness of personal power: 'Power, and the contemplation of power, in any absolute incarnation of grandeur or excess, necessarily have the instantaneous effect of quelling all perturbation' (XII, 240). Maximilian appears to him not as just a remarkable young man but as a god: 'a soldier covered with brilliant distinctions, ... radiant with the favour of courts and of Imperial ladies, ... rich beyond the dreams of romance or the necessities of a fairy tale, ... grandeur in his personal appearance ... in such excess, so far transcending anything I had ever met with in my experience, that no expectation which it is in words to raise could have been disappointed' (XII, 239). This epiphany of attractive power is followed by a series of demonic epiphanies in the form of the apparently motiveless murders of ordinary citizens which strike the city with 'the very midnight of mysterious awe' (XII, 249). The professor's narrative never suggests that the scene of these visitations is anything other than a perfectly average city, intent on its humble pursuit of daily affairs; all distinction is concentrated in a single powerful individual, all horror in the mysterious and anarchic depredations of the night. Maximilian's confessional narrative, which follows the professor's and deals with the earlier circumstances of his mother's suffering, inverts these categories as a nightmare often inverts the norms of waking experience. As a place of dungeons, tortures, and tribunals of tyrants, the city of the professor's narrative is virtually unrecognizable; destructive power has now come to be located in the repressive institutions of society itself, exercising its will through public punishments in broad day; superlative distinction is now concentrated in the helpless female representatives of an outcast race, and Maximilian himself is no more than an ineffectual boy dwelling in a 'poor house in the Jewish quarter' (XII, 279). By superimposing one frame of perspective upon its opposite De Quincey not only creates a deep ambiguity concerning the locus and the nature of omnipotence and helplessness, attractiveness and horror, but also suggests that this ambiguity is itself the deep centre of interest in the story. If De Quincey cannot rid himself in 'The Avenger' of his preoccupation with the dark Gothic demigod, he at least manipulates the frame of his narrative so as to animate another source of darkness, less glamourous, rooted in the workings of external society itself.

This process of deglamourizing, of removing any trace of omnipotence from the hero and of the exotic from the locale, reaches its full expression in 'The Household Wreck,' which, though published some six months before 'The Avenger,' represents a conceptual advance in the direction of delineating the condition of personal helplessness in a society of horror. The atmosphere of this tale, though less exotic than that of 'The Avenger,' is at the same time fundamentally disquieting. Although the central material of both works is obsessively the same (the uncomfortable triad of baleful institutional power, suffering heroine, and helpless hero), the conventions of Gothic romance in 'The Avenger' assimilate these obsessions into the literary decorum of the genre and therefore vitiate their force. 'The Household Wreck,' however, observes no literary decorum at all, neither the fixed co-ordinates of realistic or historical fiction nor the exoticism of romance. It is in fact the major example in De Quincey's art of the grotesque, that peculiar modulation of the Gothic form of which Poe is the master in English and which plays so conspicuous a role in the history of German fiction and drama since the beginning of the nineteenth century. Wolfgang Kayser, the foremost exponent of the grotesque form, alludes to its characteristic 'fusion of realms which we know to be separated, the abolition of the law of statics, the loss of identity, the distortion of "natural" size and shape' and to a sense of an 'alienation of the world' which inspires insecurity and terror.[9] The sense of sinking incoherence is a quality radically opposed to the vision of autonomous freedom which animated De Quincey's works in the early 1820s, just as the effect of nightmare thoroughly interfused with the course of ordinary life is radically opposed to the attractive grandeur of demonic power sequestered in the glamourized forms of dream and fantasy. As a capacious vessel for these new and disquieting qualities 'The Household Wreck' becomes the epitome of De Quincey's extreme vision of human impotence, and what might appear its weaknesses of plot and narration are in fact its strengths, for no other methods could provide so adequate a verbal equivalent of that vision.

Throughout the novella familiar details of everyday consciousness mingle with elements that alienate the familiar. One instance of this alienating effect appears in the peculiar ambiguity of setting; the characters are drawn from ordinary bourgeois life and have English names, but the country is itself nameless, and the period, though nominally the eighteenth century, is without distinguishing historical characteristics, so that a prominently familiar foreground is superimposed on a void. The plot itself, however, is the chief element of incongruity, as trivial circumstances of everyday life proceed to monstrous and horrifying consequences. The heroine Agnes, a young suburban housewife, ventures into the city one morning on an errand and is arrested for stealing a piece of lace from a haberdasher (it later appears that the merchant has falsified the evidence against her after she rejects his sexual advances). From such slender beginnings consequences swell in fantastic disproportion: the minister of justice of the land determines to make Agnes an example: 'all the world was agitated with the case; literally not the city only, vast as that city was, but the nation, was convulsed' (XII, 203); Agnes is sentenced to hard labour, her little son dies, her husband enters a delirium, and she herself, escaping from her dungeon, spends her miserable last days hiding in a quarter 'whither the poor only and the wretched resorted' (XII, 227), as the police close in. It is not the illogicality of this crescendo of misery that gives the plot its grotesque character (for the motif of the ravished and persecuted maiden is sufficiently conventional), but rather De Quincey's insistence upon details drawn from banal bourgeois realism: a shopping errand, a piece of lace, a haberdasher, police ledgers, details absurdly incommensurate with a pattern of events clearly drawn from Gothic romance.

Agnes is only one of a succession of Proserpina figures in De Quincey's writings, her underworld in this case composed of the 'vast, ancient, in parts ruinous, and most gloomy' prison (XII, 195) and then later the urban slums, but few such figures are given the indignity of demonic captors so prosaic as an officious civil bureaucrat and, more ludicrous, a lecherous haberdasher. It is not immediately clear whether this travesty of romance conventions is intended as some kind of joke. Whatever the intent, De Quincey appears relentless in disrupting such conventions while evoking and toying with them. Robbed of even a potential glamour in her role of ravished innocent, Agnes is also denied the conventional end of the martyr, to experience her dying moments suffused with visions of her heavenly reward. As if to enforce his bleak perspective, De Quincey does indeed afford Agnes a dream in which 'the trumpet sounded once again; and there were new heavens and a new earth' (XII, 229), but he has her awake in tears to her squalid surroundings, where she lingers wretchedly for another two months until death, described plainly and realistically (XII, 230), finally comes, unattended by further heavenly visitation. The dream of apocalypse, which was to serve De Quincey so powerfully in the visionary works of the next decade as an intimation of immortality, remains here peculiarly abortive and ambivalent, essentially an addendum to the ironic vision of the whole.

Neither the grotesque course of Agnes's story nor the character of the heroine herself, however, forms the chief centre of interest in 'The Household Wreck.' Although nominally the protagonist, Agnes is seldom observed at first hand in the story and at no point does she really assume the vividness or separate interest of a fully realized character. Instead she seems to move in a shadowy background from phase to phase of experiential woe, a wan epipsyche for the consciousness of the narrator her husband, which dominates the foreground. This consciousness flings itself forth from every page despite, or perhaps in compensation for, the narrator's virtually ineffectual role in the plot itself. It expresses itself in a massive flow of words, an agonizing retardation of narrative progress (the narrator cannot bring himself to describe the actual course of events in the story until he has presented some twenty pages of generalized lament and dire proleptic forebodings), with alternations between a fussy, laboured prosiness and eloquent rhetorical flights. 'To read it,' Edward Sackville West has said, 'is a most uncomfortable experience, not unlike listening to the elaborate complaints of a friend whom one knows to be temporarily unhinged.'[10] This comment, suggesting as it does the portrayal of a dislocated consciousness in the work, offers a satisfying insight into the bizarre style of 'The Household Wreck.'

Some passages in the work illustrate vividly incongruities of this consciousness by concentrating its extreme moods in a tense proximity:

On that day, on that lovely 6th of April, such as I have described it, – that 6th of April, about nine o'clock in the morning, – we were seated at breakfast near the open window – we, that, is, Agnes, myself, and little Francis. The freshness of morning spirits rested upon us; the golden light of the morning sun illuminated the room; the incense was floating through the air from the gorgeous flowers within and without the house. There in youthful happiness we sat gathered together, a family of love; and there we never sat again. Never again were we three gathered together, nor ever shall be, so long as the sun and its golden light, the morning and evening, the earth and its flowers, endure.

Often have I occupied myself in recalling every circumstance the most trivial of this the final morning of what merits to be called my life. Eleven o'clock, I remember, was striking when Agnes came into my study and said she would go into the city (for we lived in quite a rural suburb), that she would execute some trifling commissions which she had received from a friend in the country, and would be home again between one and two. (XII, 172–3)

The range of this passage is representative, as it moves from elegiac rhetoric in the pastoral tradition (golden light, flowers, a family of love) to the most naively bald retelling of the circumstantial details of small daily business, a baldness that comes to look obsessive in the narrator's fevered concern for pinpointing the exact moment of disaster: 'On that day, on that lovely 6th of April ... – that 6th of April, about nine o'clock in the morning'; 'eleven o'clock, I remember, was striking'; she 'would be home between one and two' – other instances of this concern with clocks occurs elsewhere in the story. The moment of severance is apparently also the moment when the harsh unyielding givens of clocks and calendars become obsessive to the narrator, a moment made more poignant by a suggestion of a different kind of time hovering in his remembrance, a time measured by the diurnal cycle of the sun with its golden lights of morning and evening. The two senses of time correspond to two kinds of memories, that of experience before severance, which is recalled only as a kind of undifferentiated bliss, its outlines softened by the elegiac tone, and that of the time of severance, and after, when the little gritty details of commonplace experience, either painful or void of imaginative resonance, become sharply etched in the consciousness. It is not inconsequential that De Quincey should show the narrator reading randomly in *Paradise Lost* on the fateful morning of Agnes's separation and hitting on the description of the parting of Adam and Eve before the temptation and Fall (XII, 184). His is an Edenic sensibility blighted by an impinging awareness of quotidian pain and bleakness. After the defeat of his innocence he has no strength left to mould his residual eloquence and his weary descriptiveness into a coherent whole.

The grotesque surface of 'The Household Wreck' undoubtedly makes the work unpleasant to read. Yet De Quincey's range of voice is greater here than in any imaginative work since the *Confessions*, and the tale is pivotal in the sequence of his works in expressing the nadir of his faith in a self-sustained imaginative power, tentatively suggested in the *Confessions* of 1822 and made central in 'The Knocking at the Gate.' The fantasized ideal of uncontrolled and even demonic power located in the self is replaced here by the ideal of attaining or recovering a fragile Edenic innocence, a dream of freedom replaced by a dream of order. Meanwhile as the self is reduced to impotence, power becomes externalized and alien to imagination, inhabiting the squalid forms of haberdasher and police minister. It is perhaps a fitting reduction of what is in some way a solipsistic ideal, and but for Margaret's death this nadir vision may not have taken shape in imaginative prose at all. For there is evidence that De Quincey was beginning in this period of his career to move beyond such baleful alternatives of solipsistic power or utter despair towards a more balanced and positive position. In the rich historical essay 'The Revolt of the Tartars' (1837), for example, he is able to view the manifestation of restless and perhaps demonic energy (which initiates the tribal revolt) both as a *self*-destructive impulse and also as a necessary first step in the regaining of an ultimate Edenic repose.[11] Such a view looks forward to De Quincey's greater productions of the 1840s, among which the *Suspiria de Profundis* of 1845 has a central place. In this work he returns at last to his original forte as a master of visionary autobiography, locating assertive strength not in external manifestations of power but in the power of his own imagination, questing for self-fulfilment and repose in a world which he ultimately finds to be one of his own making, the world of vision and dreams.

ৠ[4]ৡ

The Giant Self:
Suspiria de Profundis

There is little precedent in other major Romantic writers for the strangely late onset of De Quincey's chief phase as an imaginative artist, a phase that begins with the *Suspiria de Profundis* of his sixtieth year and continues for a dozen years more. A last and climactic bout with the powers of opium, a struggle always fecund to his imagination, partially explains this phenomenon.[1] But whatever the external circumstances, this midwinter spring of De Quincey's career is peculiarly appropriate, for a pattern of tentative beginnings and late flowering is intrinsic to all of his best work. Such a pattern is visible in the *Confessions*, for example, in the way that the common day of experience at school and in London leads to and is absorbed by the unearthly gleam of opium's revelations, or in 'The Revolt of the Tartars,' where the prosaic history of the tribe modulates into a myth of divine guidance. The phases of his literary career seem to follow the same sort of progression; it is as if De Quincey feels compelled to circle warily about his central theme of the imagination's power, occasionally approaching it and retreating, only to rush upon it at last, allowing it to transfigure his art.

Suspiria de Profundis initiates the culminating phase of this progression, and De Quincey clearly intended it to occupy a crowning place in his work. Its subtitle in the original version published in *Blackwood's Magazine* in March–July 1845 is 'A Sequel to the *Confessions of an English Opium-Eater*, and the new work supersedes, at least in intention, the earlier one that established his literary reputation. In a letter sent to his friend Professor Lushington in 1846 De Quincey calls it 'very greatly superior to the first [Confessions], ... the ne plus ultra, as regards the feeling and the power to express it, which I can ever hope to attain.'[2] Attempting to assimilate and transcend the earlier *Confessions*, the *Sus-*

piria also seems intended as a kind of repository for every piece of 'impassioned' or visionary prose that De Quincey was subsequently to write. As a list of titles found among his papers after his death indicates, he applied the general title *Suspiria de Profundis* not only to the pieces published in 1845 but also to *The English Mail-Coach* of 1849, to 'The Daughter of Lebanon,' appended to the revised *Confessions* of 1856, as well as to other pieces not published in his lifetime, some of them now lost.[3] The *Suspiria* of 1845 thus seems to represent the central core of a canonical structure, an arch of autobiography and vision, raising the life of the English opium-eater to the level of myth.[4] It is, to be sure, an unfinished arch, for De Quincey completed only one of the work's four intended sections and later raided the work freely, distributing parts of it among the heterogeneous materials gathered to form the *Autobiographic Sketches* of 1853. Yet both in its aspirations to canonical stature and in its incompleteness the *Suspiria* is reminiscent of other Romantic works of similar scope and intent such as Blake's *Four Zoas*, Wordsworth's *Recluse*, or Keats's *Hyperion*, great myths of fall and redemption which their authors can neither finish nor leave behind but which live on in successive versions of themselves. Like these, De Quincey's work is more moving for its lack of completion than any finished work could be, more revealing of the open-endedness of Romantic myth-making.

I THE 'INTRODUCTORY NOTICE'

Like Wordsworth's *Recluse*, the *Suspiria* aspires to becoming a grand philosophical poem (though in prose), marrying personal history, visionary experiences, and a universal healing doctrine. The principal difference between the two works is in their plans of organization; whereas Wordsworth expected to confine his personal history to a prefatory poem, *The Prelude*, De Quincey plans to preserve the linearity of personal narrative throughout the work, though interrupting this narrative line with presentations of vision and transcendental speculation at appropriate intervals. Thus at the end of the 'Introductory Notice' to the *Suspiria* he insists

... that the whole course of this narrative resembles, and was meant to resemble, a *caduceus* wreathed about with meandering ornaments, or the shaft of a tree's stem hung round and surmounted with some vagrant parasitical plant. The mere medical subject of the opium answers to the dry, withered pole, which shoots all the rings of the flowering plants, and seems to do so by some dexterity of its own; whereas, in fact, the plant and its tendrils have curled round the sullen cylinder by mere luxuriance of *theirs* ... The true object in my 'Opium Confessions' [De Quincy apparently means by this the *Suspiria* pieces that follow as well as his earlier work] is not the naked physiological theme ... [but] those parasitical thoughts, feelings, digressions, which climb up with bells and blossoms round about the arid stock; ramble away from it at times with perhaps too rank a luxuriance; but at the same time ... spread a glory over incidents that for themselves would be – less than nothing. (SP 157–9)

Although De Quincey is quite misleading when he speaks of 'medical subjects' and 'physiological themes' (for opium never enters the work as we have it in any medical context at all), the general meaning is plain enough. Just as the linear course of life becomes wreathed in an incremental growth of dreams, so too will the narrative line provide a central thread from which a series of digressive sorties into the imagination are to be launched. Yet some of De Quincey's language in this explanation suggests a disquieting prospect as to the formal success of such a cunning mixture of autobiographical continuity and timeless vision. The attractions of vision dangerously overbalance the interest in the life itself, which becomes a 'dry withered pole,' an 'arid stock,' 'less than nothing.' That De Quincey himself realized this danger appears from the twice-repeated reference to the 'parasitical' growth of vision upon life, a growth of 'perhaps too rank a luxuriance,' as if this growth tended to smother whatever value the depiction of a personal history might offer.

Although the formal coherence of the work may be endangered by an imbalance between its visionary and its experiential elements, a valid basis remains for the copresence and linkage of these elements. The visionary power demands experience as its precondition, and the depiction of visionary states demands autobiographical narration for a proper understanding of those states. In the *Suspiria*, as written, the pains of opium have no particular importance at all, but the splendour and grand significance of dreams everywhere receive prominence:

Among the powers in man which suffer by this too intense life of the *social* instincts, none suffers more than the power of dreaming. Let no man think this is a trifle. The machinery for dreaming planted in the human brain was not planted for nothing. That faculty, in alliance with the mystery of darkness, is the one great tube through which man communicates with the shadowy. And the dreaming organ, in connection with the heart, the eye and the ear, compose the magnificent apparatus which forces the infinite into the

chambers of a human brain, and throws dark reflections from eternities
below all life upon the mirrors of the sleeping mind. (SP 149)

As the mediating link between the finite and the infinite, between time
and eternity, the dream dignifies its creator, who temporarily houses the
infinite in his own finite corporeality, and it raises the substance of his
experience, garnered from 'the heart, the eye, and the ear,' to a higher
power, converting it into the fabric of eternal vision. Experience thus has
the growth of imagination as its goal, and transformed experience is the
subject contemplated by the developed imagination in dreams, a reciprocal relation strictly within the range of Wordsworthian conceptions,
however unlike Wordsworth De Quincey's funereal embroiderings of
the theme may be.

Given this particular strand of interest in the 'Introductory Notice,' it
is natural that some of De Quincey's most important remarks in it
should centre upon overtly Wordsworthian themes, especially the connection between meditative solitude and imaginative power.[5] The grandeur of dreams unfolds, he maintains, in inverse proportion to the
degree of one's involvement in the external multiplicities of social life,
and the familiar Wordsworthian complaint against a world too much
with us strongly enters his discussion: 'To reconcentrate [thought and
feeling] into meditative habits, a necessity is felt by all observing persons
for sometimes retiring from crowds. No man ever will unfold the capacities of his own intellect who does not at least checker his life with solitude. How much solitude, so much power' (SP 149). In this formulation
De Quincey finds the essential guidelne for the path he is to follow in the
Suspiria, particularly in the long autobiographical section of Part I, 'The
Affliction of Childhood.' His child-hero must become bereft of a primal
connection with outward things, most starkly through the loss of others
whom he loves, in order to enter a solitude which he will fill with his
imaginings. In this he is like the Wordsworthian child of the 'Intimations' ode and the 'spots of time' passages of The Prelude, who often
retires from social activities and sometimes literally becomes lost as he
moves about 'in the worlds unrealized.' The pain of life, which is loss,
and the glory of life, the power of dreaming and imagining, become
inseparably joined through the mediation of solitude, which is the outward token of pain and glory both. In this way De Quincey reconciles
the emphasis on a descent into grief and the apparently contradictory
but even more potent emphasis on an ascent out of experiential loss
into the glories of vision. Whether this reconciliation can dispel all the

formal difficulties inherent in a work that aims to proceed by rambling casually through alternative states of sequential personal history and visionary displays, it at least enables De Quincey to embark coherently on an autobiographical account that transcends personal anecdotage and aspires to the status of visionary myth.

II 'THE AFFLICTION OF CHILDHOOD'

In 'The Affliction of Childhood' De Quincey locates the crisis in his experience not at the turn between adolescence and manhood, as in the *Confessions*, but at the earliest point of conscious awareness, and hence this new autobiographical account bears a revisionary relation to his first version of personal history. The *Confessions* of 1822 takes its hero into the world of experience but allows an aura of innocence to linger about that world, so that the climactic episode, the hero's love for Ann, represents simultaneously both the culmination of this innocence and yet the goal of an arduous experiential journey. Placed at the centre of the work, this episode suggests a moment somehow in time and yet before the onset of loss and solitude. In the *Confessions* it is thus possible for innocence and connective bonds with others to assume tangible shapes in a populous world of experience. Thus Ann of Oxford Street is a realized human figure in a way that De Quincey's sister Elizabeth, the corresponding figure of lost love in the *Suspiria*, can never be, and not simply because the latter dies in childhood. The bond of love which Elizabeth shares with her brother is so confined to the remotest period of childhood and broken so early that its status in the adult's consciousness verges on the mythical and the time of its flourishing becomes Edenic. Solitude now becomes not a condition of adulthood but one that takes dominion in the earliest stages of conscious life, and almost all of De Quincey's lifetime, including his childhood, becomes empty space in which a self-sustained imagination has scope to expand. The *via negativa* towards visionary grandeur thus starts early in the *Suspiria*, rather than later, as in the *Confessions*, a sign of the *Suspiria*'s more ambitious attempt to confer a special mythic glory on autobiographical experience.

'The Affliction of Childhood' thus grants brief space to that evocation of a society dwelling in innocence, such as figured so importantly in the first half of the *Confessions*. This evocation rests simply in a modest account of the child's early background in a family comfortably supported by trade:

We, the children of the house, stood in fact, upon the very happiest tier in the scaffolding of society for all good influences. The prayer of Agar – 'Give me neither property nor riches' – was realized for us. That blessing had we, being neither too high nor too low: high enough we were to see models of good manners; obscure enough to be left in the sweetest of solitudes. Amply furnished with the nobler benefits of wealth, *extra* means of health, of intellectual culture, and of elegant enjoyment, on the other hand, we knew nothing of its social distinctions. Not depressed by the consciousness of privations too sordid, not tempted into restlessness by the consciousness of privileges too aspiring, we had no motives for shame, we had none for pride. (SP 162)

Possessing no taint of shame or pride, the environment described here suggests Eden before the Fall, the 'happy rural seat' associated in English literature from the time of Chaucer with the virtues and comforts of the provincial middle class. Moulded in such an environment by 'the gentlest of sisters, not by horrid, pugilistic brothers' (SP 163), the child dwells in a pastoral of innocence free from the intrusions of pain and strife.

The death of De Quincey's younger sister Jane disturbs this idyll, but only momentarily, for it becomes assimilated into the atmosphere of the natural pastoral in which the child continues to dwell: 'I was sad for Jane's absence. But still in my heart I trusted that she would come again. Summer and winter came again – crocuses and roses; why not little Jane?' (SP 166). If little Jane is a part of nature, the elder sister Elizabeth is like nature itself, and with the death of Elizabeth the young De Quincey seems to lose an entire world. It is important and perhaps surprising to note that, despite all his declarations of extravagant love for this sister and of grief for her loss, De Quincey presents no complete description of her, no concrete example of her virtues, and no specific instance of the affectionate regard which she is presumed to have had for her younger brother. Whatever the young boy's feeling for the actual Elizabeth may have been in 1792, the lack of circumstantial description in 'The Affliction of Childhood' enforces our sense of her representativeness, as if she were the humanized embodiment of that domestic pastoral of innocence in which De Quincey lived as a child. As his 'leader and companion' she fulfils his 'necessity of being loved' (SP 170, 169), for as leader she represents the benevolent tutelary environment, and as companion she serves as the recipient of his own emotional generosity. In this early state of the child's imaginative development transcendence is located in a human figure. In a metaphoric expression of this transcendence Elizabeth is endowed with 'a *tiara* of light or a gleaming *aureola*'; she is a 'pillar of fire,' De Quincey says, 'that didst go before me to guide and to quicken,' a 'lamp lighted in Paradise' (SP 167, 170).

The news that Elizabeth must die strikes the child like 'God's thunderbolt' (SP 171), the first manifestation of another kind of divine presence that works by power, not by love, that dwells in infinity, not concentrated in the finite human form. The second manifestation occurs when De Quincey visits the chamber where his dead sister is laid out:

Nothing met my eyes but one large window wide open, through which the sun of midsummer at noonday was showering down torrents of splendor. The weather was dry, the sky was cloudless, the blue depths seemed the express types of infinity; and it was not possible for eye to behold or for heart to conceive any symbols more pathetic of life and the glory of life. (SP 172)

The description registers a remarkable transference of qualities from the dead Elizabeth to the vivid skyscape. Life, departed from his sister, returns in emblems quintessentially 'pathetic of life'; the ineffable light which once surrounded her is replaced by the glorious light of the sun at its zenith. Somewhat later, as the child contemplates her breathless corpse, the breath returns in cosmic form in the rising swell of a 'solemn wind.' 'It was a wind that had swept the fields of mortality for a hundred centuries. Many times since, upon a summer day, when the sun is about the hottest, I have remarked the same wind arising and uttering the same hollow, solemn, Memnonian, but saintly swell: it is in this world the one sole *audible* symbol of eternity' (SP 175). In other words, the image of Elizabeth is replaced by an array of cosmic images suggesting eternal life and glory, images at once closer to inanimate nature and, in the imagination, to a divine presence than the human beloved afforded. When his sister's death removes the focal point of De Quincey's imaginative desires, they project themselves upon all of the visible cosmos, finding a more absolute expression of the infinite in a nature stripped bare of meaningful human presence.

At this point in the narrative a speculative digression intervenes. The death of a child in the fullness of June somehow strikes De Quincey's imagination as singularly appropriate, and he seeks to justify this paradoxical connection as emanating from a deep psychological principle. 'Often I have been struck with the important truth,' he says, 'that far more of our deepest thoughts and feelings pass to us through perplexed combinations of *concrete* objects, pass to us as *involutes* (if I may coin that word) in compound experiences incapable of being disentangled, than ever reach us *directly*, and in their own abstract shapes' (SP 173). This observation, manifestly relevant to the symbol-making in De Quincey's writings in general, helps to explain here the remarkable transformation that has come over the child in his sister's bedroom. In this instance Elizabeth's death in June enters an 'involute' of feeling derived from associations of Bible-reading in early childhood. These readings awakened visions of the perpetual summer of Oriental climates, visions which propagated a chain of associations: palm trees, Palm Sunday, Jerusalem, and, finally, Christ's Passion and Resurrection: 'There it was, indeed, that the human had risen on wings from the grave; but, for that reason, there also it was that the divine had been swallowed up by the abyss; the lesser star could not rise, before the greater would submit to eclipse' (SP 174–5). Three patterns of cyclic return inform the imaginative power of this involute experience: the imaginative pattern of the Christian myth, with its story of death and rebirth; the pattern of individual memory, which, in the adult writer, recovers the loves of childhood while retaining the sense of the loss of those loves; and the pattern of nature, which recreates in the stasis of summer vegetation a beauty equivocally poised in counter-processes of death and growth. The involute feeling tightly binds De Quincey's contemplation of death to a notion of resurrection; the presence of this feeling is like a privileged moment that contains all of the successive stages in a redemptive cycle simultaneously.

But these contraries are perhaps too tightly wound together, and the imaginative energy needed to hold the various elements in simultaneous juxtaposition is too demanding for the child's consciousness, which suddenly snaps and enters a trance state. The energies of imagination generated by the consciousness of contraries now propels him forward in vision on an infinite flight beyond contraries altogether:

Instantly, ... when my eye filled with the golden fulness of life, the pomps and glory of the heavens outside, and turning when it settled upon the frost which overspread my sister's face, instantly a trance fell upon me. A vault seemed to open in the zenith of the far blue sky, a shaft which ran up forever. I, in spirit, rose as if on billows that also ran up the shaft forever; and the billows seemed to pursue the throne of God; but *that* also ran before us and fled away continually. The flight and the pursuit seemed to go on for ever and ever. Frost, gathering frost, some Sarsar wind of death, seemed to repel me. (SP 176)

J. Hillis Miller, who considers the whole scene in Elizabeth's chamber as the paradigmatic depiction of the disappearance of God in De Quincey's writings, describes the deity of this passage as one 'who plays hide and seek with man, and always withdraws into a further deep of space and time as we approach closer to his throne.'[6] Although the suggestions of resurrection in the involute passage must surely qualify Miller's assessment of the whole scene as emblematic of the divine withdrawal, modern readers attuned to contemporary literature of spiritual alienation are likely to accept his view in this instance. Yet a reading derived from a Romantic context might bring to bear other associations, the Wordsworthian moment, for example,

> when the light of sense
> Goes out, but with a flash that has
> Revealed the invisible world; ...
> ... whether we be young or old,
> Our destiny, our being's heart and home,
> Is with infinitude, and only there;
> With hope it is, hope that can never die,
> Effort, and expectation, and desire,
> And something evermore about to be.
> (*The Prelude*, (II[1850], 600–8)

Geoffrey Hartman's general theory of Wordsworth's consciousness, that 'nature itself led him beyond nature'[7] to an apocalyptic awareness of the imagination's sublime autonomy, is a notion applicable as well to the progress of vision here. De Quincey's 'light of sense' is not only the summer sun 'showering down torrents of splendor' but Elizabeth herself, nature in human form, whose passing allows De Quincey an extraordinary visionary autonomy. 'The Affliction of Childhood' has thus progressed from the living light of Elizabeth to the natural but portentous light of the sky, and finally to the visionary shaft of light emanating from a God whose retreat acts as a lure to draw the spirit of the child ever farther out from the bonds of mortality. The progress patently enacts the stages of the mystic progress or 'epistrophe' from sense to spirit,[8] a point corroborated by a passage immediately following the description of the trance:

Oh flight of the solitary child to the solitary God – flight from ruined corpse to the throne that could not be ruined! – how rich wert thou in truth for after years. Rapture of grief that, being too mighty for a child to sustain, foundest

a happy oblivion in a heaven-born dream, and within that sleep didst conceal
a dream, whose meanings in after years, when slowly I deciphered, suddenly
there flashed upon me new light. (sp 176)

In a note De Quincey explicitly acknowledges his debt to Plotinus for the
first line of this passage and thus enforces the context of imaginative
quest in which the whole vision should be read. It is a context characteristically Romantic, suggestive of aspiration towards the transcendent, yet
open-ended, even tentative. The open-endedness modifies the absolut-
ism of Neoplatonic systems, but the Neoplatonic element counteracts
any tendency to interpret the vision merely as a depiction of God's
estrangement.

De Quincey's full appreciation of the vision is, however, a fruit of
'after years.' The visionary flight of the child ends on a more tentative
note. The Sarsar wind of death counters the upward surge, and whether
representing the child's mortal limitations or a sudden terror at the prospect of infinite vision (a point which De Quincey will later develop in
his essay 'System of the Heavens'), it returns him to his sister's chamber.
The suggestion of a play of contraries on a new and higher level – the
evolution of 'some mighty relation between God and death' (I, 42) –
appears only in the version of 1853. The tentativeness implies that the
visionary moment in the chamber of death is only a foretaste of the
child's imaginative development now that solitude has come upon him.
For at the funeral services he rebels at the liturgical suggestions that
Elizabeth has been transformed into a higher thing and transferred to a
better world (sp 181). His desire for the restoration of the living Elizabeth
he has known indicates a reluctance to let go of the lost domestic idyll of
innocence.

The rest of 'The Affliction of Childhood' shows the child attempting to
invest a freely roaming imagination in forms adequate to the strength of
his desire. The scenes in church which close the instalment of March
1845 provide, through architecture, picture, and music, an organizing
form to engage the imagination already diffused in the forms of nature:

The sides of the windows were rich with storied glass; through the deep
purples and crimsons streamed the golden light; emblazonries of heavenly
illumination mingling with the earthly emblazonries of what is grandest in
man ... There were the martyrs that had borne witness to the truth through
flames ... There were the saints who, under intolerable pangs, had glorified
God by meek submission to his will. (sp 185)

This scene offers more than the solace to be gained from moralizing depictions. The beauties of natural light and human art join in the stained glass to cancel the martyrs' pain, though they do so by augmenting its visual intensity. Once again, as in Elizabeth's chamber, an externally presented involute of contrary elements prompts the child's own visionary efforts. Awakened by the pictorial art of the stained glass, the imaginative eye of the child paints a story of its own making upon the vision of clouds and sky, glimpsed through the central window where the glass is clear; the clouds become beds of dying children, and their drift through the sky becomes an ascent into the heavens, where a benevolent God, no longer retreating, reaches down to meet them (SP 186).

As a visionary experience this is inadequate; not only is the conversion of clouds into beds mechanical (and visually most awkward), but, unlike the earlier trance, there is no flight of the visionary child towards God, only the sentimental piety of levitating children observed by an earthbound eye. What the child has created is another pictorial exemplum, and the power of simple pictorial projection is beginning to interfere with more sophisticated modes of imagination. Fortunately during the whole creation of this visual experience another form of art is present, the tumultuous music pouring from the church organ:

But not the less the blare of the tumultuous organ wrought its own separate creations. And oftentimes in anthems, when the mighty instrument threw its vast columns of sound, fierce yet melodious, over the voices of the choir – when it rose high in arches, as might seem, surmounting and overriding the strife of the vocal parts, and gathering by strong coercion the total storm into unity – sometimes I seemed to walk triumphantly upon those clouds which so recently I had looked up to as mementos of prostrate sorrow, and even as ministers of sorrow in its creations; yes, sometimes under the transfigurations of music I felt of grief itself as of a fiery chariot for mounting victoriously above the causes of grief. (SP 186)

As in so many Romantic works the ear proves mightier than the eye, and this time it is the child who rises, not the objects of his vision. The visual display of the windows, even the display of ascending children shown to the inner eye, are prefigurative visions, pointing to the child's ultimate unification with God in some indefinite future. But music is reflexive rather than figurative in significance; it moves towards the unification of its own self-created oppositions independent of any external reference, and thus can function as the precise equivalent of the free imagination's self-fulfilling operation, made sensually manifest to the child for the first time. In its temporal aspect it carries the child, like Elijah, to the triumphant consummation of those portents first glimpsed in the chamber of his sister; in its spatial aspects, both actual (the locations of choir and organ in the church) and metaphoric (the 'vast columns of sound,' 'high in arches'), it becomes the very architectural structure of the heavenly mansion imaginatively attained.

The experience in church, resolves, in a limited fashion, the paradoxical nature of the visionary flight undertaken in the young De Quincey's first trance. There his imagination sought fulfilment in a goal of absolute transcendence, the throne of God, but this goal is unattainable in any finite quest, though it is this unavailability that guarantees the increase of the child's autonomous imaginative strength. The church and its music at last provide a locus of outward forms to engage and absorb the imaginative energies liberated by the loss of Elizabeth. Yet this receptive function in no way diminishes the autonomy of the child's solitary quest, for the music spells out in sound a self-renewing movement of imagination that is intrinsically his own. Though music carries the child on a chariot of sound, as earlier the billows of his trance carried him towards the throne of God, the vehicle here is the glory attained, a self-fulfilled sublimity. The vehicle none the less still remains external to his imagination, and since the boy cannot remain forever in church, a dangerous freedom returns as his imagination once more roams in solitude. 'Solitude, though silent as light, is, like light, the mightiest of agencies; for solitude is essential' (SP 188). This is beautiful but disquieting, and it is not surprising that it begins to turn into a death-wish, a longing for the ultimate solitude disguised as reunion:

... There is a necessity that, if too much left to itself in solitude, finally [grief] will descend into a depth from which there is no reascent: into a disease which seems no disease; into a languishing which, from its very sweetness, perplexes the mind, and is fancied to be very health. Witchcraft has seized upon you – nympholepsy has struck you. Now you rave no more. You acquiesce; nay, you are passionately delighted in your condition. Sweet becomes the grave, because you hope immediately to travel thither.   (SP 196–7)

Such a repose would be a denial of the imaginative quest altogether, and it is a sign of imaginative strength that the child soon turns away from this preoccupation.

The turning away involves putting on 'the harness of life' (SP 199) and entering into the normal routine of ordinary childhood occupations, as described in the April 1845 issue of *Blackwood's*. The problem of an unfixed imaginative excess still remains, and it becomes an aesthetic problem for De Quincey as author as well as an existential problem for the child. 'The Affliction of Childhood' begins at this point to move with a disastrous wobble, mingling eloquent apostrophes to the imaginative and moral capacities of children with anecdotes that belong in the nursery. The 'heart overflowing with love' (SP 203) now invests its bounty of grief upon the penning up of Newfoundland dogs and the deaths of kittens and kitchen spiders (SP 199 – 206). It becomes apparent that De Quincey does not know what to do with his visionary theme while pursuing his commitment to a consecutive account of the 'arid stock' of his ordinary life experiences. The theme of imagination is either an obstacle to a truly interesting account of childhood episodes, or, as is more likely, these episodes simply are inadequate to De Quincey's increasing concern, the quest for a fulfilling visionary experience.

Thus a new official direction for the work becomes established openly as 'The Affliction of Childhood' draws to a close, a direction which corresponds to the types of cyclic return, glimpsed in the involute experiences in Elizabeth's chamber:

Ups and downs you will see, heights and depths, in our fiery course together, such as will sometimes tempt you to look shyly and suspiciously at me, your guide, and the ruler of the oscillations. Here ... the reader has reached the lowest depths in my nursery afflictions. From that point, according to the principles of *art* which govern the movement of these Confessions, I had meant to launch him upwards through the whole arch of ascending visions which seemed requisite to balance the sweep downwards, so recently described in his course.   (SP 222)

The 'lowest depths' mentioned here are merely the trivial sorrows of the nursery, and one begins to wonder 'shyly and suspiciously' how much 'descent' has actually occurred in 'The Affliction of Childhood'. Having paid his dues to anecdotal autobiography, the 'ruler of the oscillations' feels no compunction in leaping an interval of twelve years in order to arrive at Oxford and the youth's first experience with opium. Opium brings on dreams that arrest the reverberations of experiences previously described and reconstitute them with greater intensity:

Again I was in the chamber with my sister's corpse, again the pomps of life rose up in silence, the glory of summer, the frost of death. Dream formed itself mysteriously within dream; within these Oxford dreams remoulded itself continually the trance in my sister's chamber ... Once again arose the swell of the anthem, the burst of the Hallelujah chorus, the storm, the trampling movement of the choral passion, the agitation of my own trembling sympathy, the tumult of the choir, the wrath of the organ. Once more I, that wallowed, became he that rose up to the clouds. And now in Oxford all was bound up into unity; the first state and the last were melted into each other as in some sunny glorifying haze.   (SP 224–5)

As 'The Affliction of Childhood' returns to its point of departure, the celebration of the grandeur of dreams, the rationale of this autobiographical narration becomes clear. It traces not only an increasingly insistent desire for transcendence but also an increasing awareness in the imaginer that the location of this transcendence lies within himself, within the spectrum of his own experience. As a product of his own imagination and a recapitulation of his own past, the dream testifies to the grandeur of the dreamer, not of some external absolute. Yet it is as final a reward as union with that retreating figure of an absolute God would have been, for the dreamer views his own past transfigured into a consummate pattern, in which the 'first state and the last,' like the apocalyptic Alpha and Omega, are bound together in unity. In these dreams the very capacity for vision becomes the subject of vision ('Dream formed within dream') and every moment of discovered pattern, every involute glimpsed along the way, becomes a prophetic microcosm of this encompassing pattern which the imagination fulfils for itself. In this way the youth's quest ends not in some otherworldly attainment but in a state which repeats the events of the quest itself and raises them to a higher power. At this point De Quincey is impelled to abandon autobiographical continuity in order to elaborate on the metaphysics of his discovery, enlarging its significance by projecting it through metaphor and myth. Suspiria de Profundis now changes from a work describing the growth of the visionary faculty in an individual to one in which the products of this growth are set forth for all to behold.

III MYTHS OF THE GIANT SELF

The four semi-didactic, semi-visionary prose-poems which conclude Part I of Suspiria de Profundis repeat, amplify, and summarize themes that have appeared before. Each piece forms an independent and self-sufficient variation on the theme of the whole, and De Quincey suggests that together they 'may be viewed as in the nature of choruses winding up the overture contained in Part I' (SP 236). *Suspiria de Profundis* obviously aspires in some way to the condition of music, as if the whole work were an attempted expansion in words of its own central emblem, the grand organ concert first heard in the church services and then reheard in dreams. In this kind of autobiography the 'chorus' of set-pieces performs a function corresponding to that of dreams in the subject's life: while it teaches that living experience deploys itself in an aesthetic pattern, it is in itself the climax of the pattern. The dream provides the visionary synthesis that testifies to the subject's strength of imagination and rescues him from an absurd condition composed of banality and fruitless pain; the prose-poems likewise rescue autobiographical narrative from its potential tendency to submerge thematic interest in an accumulation of trivial incident and detail.

The starting-point for the expanding circles of speculation that pervade these pieces lies in De Quincey's notion of the connection between early experiences of sorrow and a compensatory grandeur of imaginative power in later life. In this latter part of the *Suspiria* De Quincey neither forgets the loss of his sister nor lets us forget it, as frequent allusions to 'the deep, deep tragedies of infancy' (SP 236) make plain. Nevertheless his main concern with the resulting personal gain is even more apparent here than it was in 'The Affliction of Childhood.' In a piece called 'The Dark Interpreter,' apparently written for the *Blackwood's* series of 1845 and then discarded, De Quincey seems to regard the experience of loss as a kind of moral and psychological tonic to strengthen his own development: 'Pain driven to agony, or grief driven to frenzy, is essential to the ventilation of profound natures ... A nature which is profound in excess but also introverted in excess, so as to be in peril of wasting itself in interminable reverie, cannot be awakened sometimes without afflictions that go to the very foundations, heaving, stirring, yet finally harmonizing.'[9] In the 'Finale' of Part I, 'Savannah-la-Mar,' an even more ambitious role is assigned to grief, one that confirms the implicit movement of the *Suspiria* away from contemplation of the loveliness of the vanished past and towards the prospective grandeur of the self: 'O, deep is the plowing of grief! But oftentimes less would not suffice for the agriculture of God. Upon a night of earthquake he builds a thousand years of pleasant habitations for man. Upon the sorrow of an infant he raises oftentimes from human intellects glorious vintages that could not else have been' (SP

255–6). These suggestions of a millennium founded upon cataclysm, peculiarly Blakean in their combination of agricultural and apocalyptic imagery, are now appropriated to the history of the self. They strikingly indicate the scope of De Quincey's aspirations as nothing less audacious than the attainment of transcendence and spiritual resurrection in this life, an attainment based upon a knowing of all the modes of human experience. This is made explicit in the most programmatic of the *Suspiria* pieces, 'Levana and Our Ladies of Sorrow,' in which the allegorical Ladies, each representing a phase of De Quincey's personal history, proclaim the purpose of their stern influence over him: 'So shall he be accomplished in the furnace, so shall he see the things that ought *not* to be seen, sights that are abominable, and secrets that are unutterable. So shall he read elder truths, sad truths, grand truths, fearful truths. So shall he rise again *before* he dies. And so shall our commission be accomplished which from God we had – to plague his heart until we had unfolded the capacities of his spirit' (SP 246). De Quincey italicizes 'before' explicitly to dissociate this rising from the traditional Christian ascent out of the earthly vale of tears, an ascent which is of course postmortem. De Quincey gives his official allegiance to Christianity, but his imagination is at all times Romantic in its metaphysics and thus frequently revisionary in its relation to orthodox beliefs.

One example of this spiritual rising before death has already appeared in the *Suspiria*, the opium-dreams at Oxford described at the end of 'The Affliction of Childhood,' dreams which recapitulate past experience, render it synchronic, and cast over it 'some sunny glorifying haze' of transfiguration. In the prose-poems that follow the 'The Affliction of Childhood' the focus of De Quincey's attention begins to shift from the theme of grief *per se* to this visionary power of perceiving the diachronic order of personal experience as a synchronic pattern. It is a pattern so radiant in its unity and balance that to contemplate it is in itself the glory and reward of experience, the resurrection of the spirit in this life. In 'The Palimpsest,' the first of the four pieces which conclude Part I, De Quincey compares this mode of perception to the phenomenon of the palimpsest manuscript, an objective record of successive pasts gathered together upon a single surface:

In our own heaven-created palimpsest, the deep memorial palimpsest of the brain, there are not and cannot be ... incoherencies. The fleeting accidents of a man's life and its external shows may indeed be irrelate and incongruous; but the organizing principles which fuse into harmony, and gather about fixed predetermined centres, whatever heterogeneous elements life may have accumulated from without, will not permit the grandeur of human unity greatly to be violated, or its ultimate repose to be troubled, in the retrospect from dying moments, or from other great convulsions. (SP 233)

The homing tendency of the 'fleeting accidents' of life, propagated by the journey of experience, finally make that journey self-justifying; in the palimpsest of retrospective vision, the 'grandeur of human unity' is inseparably linked to the proliferation of past experiences, as their traces left on the memory at last converge.

An anecdote from 'The Palimpsest' describing the reported visions of a child on the point of drowning vividly communicates the theory of the simultaneity of the past and the glory conferred on those who behold this pattern:

At a certain stage of [her] descent, a blow seemed to strike her, phosphoric radiance sprang forth from her eyeballs; and immediately a mighty theatre expanded within her brain. In a moment, in the twinkling of an eye, every act, every design of her past life, lived again, arraying themselves not a succession, but as parts of a coexistence. Such a light fell upon the whole path of her life backwards into the shades of infancy, as the light, perhaps, which wrapt the destined Apostle on his road to Damascus. Yet that light blinded for a season; but hers poured celestial vision upon the brain, so that her consciousness became omnipresent at one moment to every feature in the infinite review. (SP 234–5)

What is striking about this passage is not the commonplace notion that drowning people see their whole lives flash before their eyes, but that emphasis upon light and expanded vision: 'phosphoric radiance,' 'celestial vision,' 'a mighty theatre expanding,' 'infinite review.' The implied comparison of the child's vision to that of St Paul is especially bold; the apostle is blinded, but the child's vision becomes clear and god-like, 'celestial' and 'omnipresent'; and the radiance emanating from one's individual life seen as a whole becomes implicitly parallel to the radiance emanating from Christ. Such a passage, describing the discovery of incarnate divinity in the depths of the self, remarkably inverts the young boy's vision in the chamber of his dead sister. In the former vision there was an ascent into the heavens in pursuit of a retreating God, but here there is a descent into translucent depths to find an adequate divinity in the totality of self-discovery.

Behind the overt double-myth of the four visionary pieces – the diachronic myth of experiential loss and imaginative resurrection, the synchronic myth of life seen as a multi-faceted design in a moment of total apprehension – there is yet another that encompasses these.[10] This myth, not stated directly, is deducible from the series of metaphors that express the overt themes. The sequence of images that, each in its turn, dominates the four pieces tells a tale of its own, indeed the only tale of which we can share the experience, for the dreamer's experience of the mystic moment of simultaneity is really unavailable to us in literary form. Our vision, instead, is of a palimpsest manuscript, three majestic Ladies of Sorrow, a giant form projected against the sky, a great city drowned by God and explored by human vision. The three latter images all involve grand personified figures of mysterious power, and the first and last present images of multifoliate forms, the work of many generations of hands. All of these images have as their common denominator the sensed presence of a giant composite form, at once human and divine, like Blake's universal man, Albion, one who incorporates past, present, and future, and of whom each individual man is a microcosm.[11] Such a myth makes comprehensible De Quincey's glorification of the pattern of the individual life as apolcalyptic, a glorification that might otherwise seem solipsistic and unearned. In 'The Palimpsest of the Human Brain' the myth is presented obliquely, although the anecdote about the drowning child approaches it more openly; 'Levana and Our Ladies of Sorrow' and 'The Apparition of the Brocken' present directly dream-visions of giant, archetypal figures; and 'Savannah-la-Mar' combines some of the obliquity of 'The Palimpsest' with direct invocations of the power of human vision and divine order. The first of these pieces offers in the image of the palimpsest not the presence of the Giant Man himself but the cumulative record of his imaginative products as seen in the successive stages of literary development:

In the illustration imagined by myself, from the case of some individual palimpsest, the Grecian tragedy had seemed to be displaced, but was *not* displaced, by the monkish legend; and the monkish legend had seemed to be displaced, but was *not* displaced, by the knightly romance. In some potent convulsion of the system, all wheels back into its earliest elementary stage. The bewildering romance, light tarnished with darkness, the semi-fabulous legend, truth celestial mixed with human falsehoods, these fade even of themselves, as life advances. The romance has perished that the young man adored; the legend has gone that deluded the boy; but the deep, deep tragedies of infancy ... these remain lurking below all, and these lurk to the last. (SP 235–6)

The various literary forms recovered from the palimpsest – Attic tragedy, a saint's life, and chivalric romance – are all close in outlook and derivation to a religious or mythic consciousness, and they represent successive stages of its development in the Western poetic tradition. De Quincey skilfully associates the various stages of individual human development (particularly his own) with those of the imagination as it unfolds in history: the feeling of primal loss with pagan tragedy, the imaginative religiosity of the child with devotional legend, the questing impulse of the youth with romance.[12] The history of the individual imagination is thus a microcosm of the history of imagination in general, itself a giant organic form with perpetually accessible origins.

The metaphor of the giant figure becomes explicit in the next piece, 'Levana and Our Ladies of Sorrow,' now made personal in import, though grandly transcending the significance of De Quincey's own private woes. The figure of Levana, the Roman goddess of childhood education, becomes representative of the whole process of a resurrection of the spirit through the experience of grief (SP 238), and her ministers, the three Ladies of Sorrow, similarly become Romantic analogues of ancient and traditional mythic forces: 'these are the Sorrows; and they are three in number, as the *Graces* are three, who dress man's life with beauty: the *Parcae* are three, who weave the dark arras of man's life in their mysterious loom always with colors sad in part, sometimes angry with tragic crimson and black; the *Furies* are three, who visit with retributions called from the other side of the grave offenses that walk upon this' (SP 239). For De Quincey sorrow represents his fate and his nemesis, but it also holds for him the grace of an elegiac beauty that inspires his song. These figures thus associate the various influential powers of traditional myth with a power of special significance to the writer as an individual. Furthermore, it appears that each of them is representative of a phase of De Quincey's own life. Thus the first of the Sorrows, the *Mater Lachrymarum* corresponds to the period of childhood loss and to a religion-haunted landscape: 'And I knew by childish memories that she could go abroad upon the winds, when she heard that sobbing of litanies, or the thundering of organs, and when she beheld the mustering of summer clouds' (SP 241). The second, the *Mater Suspiriorum*, is associated with what De Quincey calls 'The Pariah Worlds,' the unredeemed present of terrestrial wandering and imprisonment in time; and the third, the *Mater Tenebra-*

rum, with 'The Kingdom of Darkness,' the realm where the dreamer shall see 'the things that ought *not* to be seen, sights that are abominable, and secrets that are unutterable' (SP 246). This dark kingdom is apparently the apocalyptic realm of demonic horror, not described directly in the *Suspiria* but already described in 'The Pains of Opium' in the *Confessions* of 1822.

Evidently to fix precisely the symbolic significance of these figures is not an easy task. They are deities or influential presences, avatars of the ancient Graces, Furies, Fates, and Muses all coalesced, and at the same time they are allegorical emblems representing successive temporal phases of an individual consciousness, as well as actual dream images (SP 240). If they signify, in discursive terms, the operative forces that enable De Quincey to attain a visionary imagination, in so far as they appear in the actual verbal presentation they are themselves the vision that we behold:

But the third sister, who is also the youngest! Hush! whisper whilst we talk of *her*! Her kingdom is not large, or else no flesh should live; but within that kingdom all power is hers. Her head, turreted like that of Cybèle, rises almost beyond the reach of sight. She droops not; and her eyes rising so high *might* be hidden by distance. But, being what they are, they cannot be hidden; through the treble veil of crape which she wears, the fierce light of a blazing misery, that rests not for matins or for vespers, for noon of day or noon of night, for ebbing or for flowing tide, may be read from the very ground.   (SP 244)

This description of the *Mater Tenebrarum* clearly does not reduce the figure to a mere emblem for a discursive equivalent of, say, opium addiction. All of De Quincey's considerable stylistic powers – the insistent prose rhythms, the parallels and antitheses, the striking pictorial details (the towering headdress, the blazing eyes) – certainly direct the reader here to more than a mundane understanding of an allegorical figure. They evoke, rather, a sharing of the writer's awe before his own visionary creation of a giant power. Although the outline of 'Levana and Our Ladies of Sorrow' is programmatic, the piece fulfils itself in generating huge and mighty forms whose power to fascinate is autonomous even if their source is in the phases of the writer's personal experience.

The emergence of the Giant Man as the true hero of the *Suspiria* is clarified in 'The Apparition of the Brocken.' This piece describes an imaginary ascent of the Brocken, a mountain in North Germany, where, under certain atmospheric conditions, spectators may observe gigantic silhouettes of themselves projected against distant mountains and clouds. The ascent takes place on Whitsunday, which commemorates the pentecostal visit of the Holy Spirit to the apostles and suggests an inspiration even more hallowed than that bestowed by Levana and her ministers. This hallowed ascent, however, reveals not the traditional vision of the celestial spheres but rather a vision of the self writ large upon them. As the projected figure mimics the actions of the observer, 'you are now satisfied,' De Quincey says, 'that the apparition is but a reflex of yourself; and, in uttering your secret feelings to *him*, you make this phantom the dark symbolic mirror for reflection to the daylight what else must be hidden forever' (SP 251). Like the Ladies of Sorrow, the Brocken apparition is both a projection of the self and a mythic giant; he is a protean figure who mimics the actions of all who ascend the mountain, one who reflects the motions of grief and Christian devotion on Whitsunday but who has also reflected in ages past the 'bloody rites' of Druidism once performed on the summit of the mountain (SP 249). De Quincey thus associates the apparition not only with the private world of the individual dreamer but also with the larger sphere of man's typological consciousness, the human imagination which has been able to encompass the horror of demonic idolatry and the repose of Christian peace.

The myth of the giant form, for which the Brocken spectre is a convenient external emblem, finds its internal reflection in the figure of the Dark Interpreter, who appears in De Quincey's dreams:

He is originally a mere reflex of my inner nature. But as the apparition of the Brocken sometimes is disturbed by storms or by driving showers, so as to dissemble his real origin, in like manner the Interpreter sometimes swerves out of my orbit, and mixes a little with alien natures. I do not always know him in these cases as my own parhelion. What he says, generally, is but that which *I* have said in daylight, and in meditation deep enough to sculpture itself on my heart. But sometimes, as his face alters, his words alter; and they do not always seem such as I have used, or *could* use. (SP 251)

The Dark Interpreter is primarily the voice of the self in dreams, that inevitable 'I' who is their protagonist, but he maintains an 'otherness' that removes him from full identity with the dreamer.[13] His utterances are unrecognizable, not because they conform to a Freudian notion of desires forbidden to the knowledge of the conscious self, but because he represents the dreamer's imagination at the outer verge of its individuality, at the point of transaction with large and autonomous powers which assert their presence in the sleeping mind.

The clear image of the giant form achieved in 'The Apparition of the Brocken' is disturbed by the complexity of the 'Finale: Savannah-la-Mar,' which in its attempt to sweep all the major preceding themes of the *Suspiria* into its brief compass offers a difficulty scarcely matched elsewhere in De Quincey's writings. As the action of the *Suspiria* starts in effect with 'God's thunderbolt,' his removal of Elizabeth, in 'Savannah-la-Mar' the work returns in an enormously magnified way to its origins:

God smote Savannah-la-mar, and in one night, by earthquake, removed her, with all her towers standing and population sleeping, from the steadfast foundations of the shore to the coral floors of ocean. And God said, – 'Pompeii did I bury and conceal from men through seventeen centuries: this city I will bury, but not conceal. She shall be a monument to men of my mysterious anger, set in azure light through generations to come; for I will enshrine her in a crystal dome of my tropic seas.' This city, therefore, like a mighty galleon with all her apparel mounted, streamers flying, and tackling perfect, seems floating along the noiseless depths of ocean; and oftentimes in glassy calms, through the translucid atmosphere of water that now stretches like an air-woven awning above the silent encampment, mariners from every clime look down into her courts and terraces, count her gates, and number the spires of her churches. She is one ample cemetery, and *has* been for many a year; but in the mighty calms that brood for weeks over tropic latitudes, she fascinates the eye with a *Fata-Morgana* revelation, as of human life still subsisting in submarine asylums sacred from the storms that torment our upper air. (SP 253–4)

Savannah-la-Mar in its submerged state is the coalesced form of many opposites reconciled in a harmonious balance, an involute like the death-in-summer described in 'The Affliction of Childhood.' It has the multitudinousness of a city – courts and terraces, gates and spires – tempered, however, by silence, stasis, and the soft monochromatic suffusions of 'azure light.' Forever fixed and stationary, it seems to float like a galleon; the waters that cover it become an 'atmosphere,' a 'crystal dome,' like an 'air-woven awning' or second sky; an 'ample cemetery,' it suggests 'human life still subsisting'; the product of cataclysm and 'mysterious anger,' it has now become an asylum 'sacred from the storms that torment our upper air.' If the city has experienced a death in summer, it is now a summer-in-death, as its location in the eternal warmth of the tropics fittingly suggests.

On one level De Quincey's dream-descent to Savannah-la-Mar, accompanied by the Dark Interpreter, is a descent to a transformed memory of his dead sister, for it was her passing that generated the mutually involved associations of death and summer, descent into the grave and visionary ascent through a 'translucid atmosphere.' The image of the sunken city combines these associations, as it curiously combines associations of the corpse of the beloved and the paradisal city which receives her; like the New Jerusalem of Revelation, Savannah-la-Mar is to some degree 'a city yet a woman' (note De Quincey's use of feminine pronouns in referring to it). More oviously, of course, it is an elaborated version of the 'mighty theatre' of the past recaptured, seen by the drowning girl in the 'Palimpsest' anecdote, an image of the variety of life arrayed in a simultaneous order. It becomes a vision of the past as life englobed in crystal, and hence the dreamer's descent may also suggest a visionary return to his own past experience, harmonized by the ordering powers of imagination. But autobiographical associations are scarcely overt in this vision, and the clear resemblance of Savannah-la-Mar to Atlantis and other lost golden isles symbolizing the happy spot of early days universalizes its significance.[14] Most generally, then, Savannah-la-Mar suggests a synthesis of all pasts, once existing vitally in time, now Edenic in the mythic memory, and this memory is like the covering waters, separating yet joining the 'here-and-now' surface and the deep visionary image.

De Quincey's image of the drowned city becomes in its own way a kind of giant form, an inclusive emblem for the totality of human productions and desires, fusing disguised references to personal memory with allusions to ultimate losses and hopes on a universal scale.[15] It is, to be sure, a passive version of this form, a product and not a producer, and in this sense it differs from the images of the Ladies of Sorrow and the Brocken apparition. Those figures function simultaneously as referential emblems for the products of experience and as visionary depictions of a giant power, the creative force behind experience, but in 'Savannah-la-Mar' De Quincey separates the emblems of the desired and the desirer, the created and the creative. The creative role falls partially to the dreamer and his double, the Dark Interpreter, who are privileged to explore the drowned city and philosophize definitively upon its significance, but the ultimate creative force in the work is that God whose giant power and mysterious purpose bring Savannah-la-Mar to its present state of timeless repose.

'Creative' may seem an inappropriate term to apply to a power that operates by visitations of destruction, and the Dark Interpreter seeks to explain God's plan by a rather enigmatic argument concerning the relation between human and divine time:

The time which *is* contracts into a mathematic point; and even that point persists a thousand times before we can utter its birth. All is finite in the present; and even that finite is infinite in its velocity of flight towards death. But in God there is nothing finite; but in God there is nothing transitory; but in God there *can* be nothing that tends to death. Therefore, it follows, that for God there can be no present. The future is the present of God, and to the future it is that he sacrifices the human present. Therefore it is that he works by earthquake. Therefore it is that he works by grief.   (SP 255)

All of this may simply mean that God destroys man in order to bring him to heaven all the sooner, but the vision of the drowned city provides associations which enrich and transfigure so bald a formulation. Savannah-la-Mar dwells in a time that is not, a suspended state that incorporates past and future, death and living beauty, a prophetic facsimile for the dreamer of that vision of eternity which awaits the whole cosmos when the present of man and the present of God shall be one. But as a living, terrestrial city every moment of its existence rushed it towards that moment of pure disaster when before and after fell away into non-being. The same melancholy situation confronts every man in so far as he is subject to the anxieties of time-bound existence; each present moment of existence is like a last stand on rapidly shrinking ground, a stand on the brink of two abysses, a past which is all loss and a future which is all threat. But in the divine present of God the perspective is quite different, for the abyss is filled with healing and preserving waters that invest the entire corpus of time with a harmonious beauty. If the human future is the present of God, then it follows that our present must be for him the past, not of course in the sense that it is a memorial record of his experience, but in the way that a narrative written in the past tense must seem to its author, beyond contingency when completed, yet with all its events copresent in the sheaves of pages that comprise it.

When Savannah-la-Mar awakes at last so that its bells and organs 'will utter a *jubilate* repeated by the echoes of Paradise' (SP 254), the event will signal an end to all contingency, the moment when, as J. Hillis Miller has said, 'all presents have flowed into the past' and the whole course of human history arrays itself as a timeless presence.[16] God is thus the supreme artist, and his acts of destruction are in fact acts of creation ('Therefore he works by grief'), for they release events from the anxieties of time so that they may take their place in a panorama of incomparable beauty. It should be clear now how relevant this divine activity is to De Quincey's belief in the beautiful simultaneity of events as seen in dreams and vision. The divine vision of human history is precisely analogous to the dreamer's vision of the sunken city, the metropolis of human contingencies which has undergone a sea-change into a panorama of perfection, and every such vision of the past in the *Suspiria* is a type of the divine vision. If the personal past, the cumulative product of the individual's loves and acts, is a microcosm of the giant and cumulative product of all human experience, the shaping imagination that endows that product with beauty is a microcosm of the giant form of God's imagination. De Quincey becomes the power he is seeking, rising before he dies not so much as one saved, but as one saving, as the artist who can make us see the vicissitudes of human life through the integrating faculties of the divine eye.

The essential thematic design of Part I of the *Suspiria* is now complete; it traces the story of an imagination which, having lost the beloved human figure in whom it originally invested its entire strength, reaches out in search of new rooting, finding it first in the church music, then in the Oxford dreams, and finally in the literary myth of a giant self. In the self-evident art of the visionary *Suspiria* pieces, with their intricate subtleties of argument and metaphor and their sonorities of verbal music, this myth of capable power becomes a reality. The design is Wordsworthian in its beginnings, for Wordsworth's early 'spots of time' involve almost entirely moments of sundering or sudden discontinuity with a consequent release of psychic energy. In its later phases, however, the design of the *Suspiria* acquires something of a Blakean character; it becomes increasingly concerned with the individual poet's imagination and experience as a microcosm of the whole of human existence, viewed as timeless in the divine vision (although De Quincey's visionary impulse, unlike Blake's, is quite devoid of ethical concerns and aspires toward a quite un-Blakean attainment of final stasis).

Although this movement from Wordsworthian to Blakean modes (to label them conveniently) gives to Part I of the *Suspiria* a powerful effect of crescendo, the balance of autobiographical concerns and yearnings for apocalyptic vision poses great danger to the unity and even the feasibility of the *Suspiria de Profundis* as a projected whole. The visions which bring

Part I to its climax prophesy the attainment of a state where the pattern of the individual life and the pattern of the universal vision become equivalent, but in order to demonstrate this equivalence and not merely to assert it De Quincey must work his way through the rest of his autobiographical history, through the 'Pariah Worlds' and the 'Kingdom of Darkness.' The visionary luxuriance of the climactic prose-poems of Part I makes it easy to forget that the personal narrative has brought us only to De Quincey's middle childhood, to which it must return rather anticlimactically. De Quincey's eagerness to display his visionary and metaphysical pattern causes him to present the climax too soon, or else the 'Finale' of Part I is not really a finale, but only a visionary way-station, as it were, on the course of a continuing autobiographical narrative, with the true culmination yet to come. But what can any such vision offer that has not been offered already, what can surpass the apocalyptic theodicy of 'Savannah-la-Mar'? In the '*caduceus*' passage from the 'Introductory Notice' De Quincey has promised 'digressions, which climb up with bells and blossoms round the arid stock [of personal history], ramble away from it at times with perhaps too rank a luxuriance'; is this an indication that each of the four projected parts of the *Suspiria* is to receive its own crowning wreath of metaphysical speculations and visions? It is difficult to guess how such a plan could be managed without awkwardness and redundance. The problem is fundamental; De Quincey's commitment to autobiographical continuity and his fascination with transcendent vision, however intrinsically connected on the thematic level, war with one another on the aesthetic level and cripple the potential of the *Suspiria* to fulfil its own thematic postulates.

In the somewhat shapeless and perhaps fragmentary second part of the *Suspiria*, called 'The Vision of Life,' De Quincey conscientiously attempts to continue the story of his youth with anecdotes about his days at school, which he later transfers, rightly, to the *Autobiographic Sketches* of 1853. It is in some ways an altogether fresh start, for it dissociates itself from the theme of Part I, the visionary return of the past, and directs its interest towards a more conventionally autobiographical theme, the progressive development of personal experience in ordinary life. The new emphasis appears in a remark that 'as "in to-day already walks to-morrow," so in the past experience of a youthful life may be seen dimly the future' (SP 258). This 'past experience' is now prologue not to visionary triumphs but to events surmised 'in troubled vision, by a young man who stands upon the threshold of manhood' (SP 258), scenes of 'the *strife* which besets us, strife from conflicting opinions, positions, passions, interests' (SP 259). The future, not the past, now becomes the arena of suffering, and dream-visions not published in De Quincey's lifetime, such as 'The Princess and the Pomegranate' and 'Who is this Woman That Beckoneth and Warneth Me,' both dealing with ominous portents of the future, may have been intended as part of another 'chorus' of visionary pieces designed to suit this portion of the *Suspiria*.[17] De Quincey's imagination cannot shake itself free, however, of the memory of beautiful and suffering female figures, and he concludes 'The Vision of Life,' not with a narration of his masculine hero engaging in the strife of the world, but with a rambling account of three generations of lovely women, blighted by disease and unrequited love. The ostensible excuse for this account is to show 'the past viewed not *as* the past, but by a spectator who steps back ten years deeper into the rear, in order that he may regard it as a future' (SP 278), an aim which associates the anecdote with the general emphasis in Part II. In fact, however, De Quincey shows himself far less interested in experimenting with a temporal point of view than in multiplying wilted flowers as a sentimental indulgence. This dismal straying from the course suggests strongly that De Quincey is either bored with the task of providing a detailed account of his life or uncertain of the value such an account might have.

Significantly *Suspiria de Profundis* never appeared anywhere in the Collective Edition published in De Quincey's lifetime, and in the final version, which according to its publisher in 1871 had received the 'benefit of the Author's revision and correction' (XIII, 333), all traces of autobiographical narrative including 'The Affliction of Childhood' itself have been removed, leaving only the dream-visions and metaphysical speculations. But even in 1845 De Quincey's eye is clearly fixed upon the glamour of the visionary experience, a glamour that dims the ordinary events of personal history. In the next few years of his literary career the interest in self-exploration is to become submerged or deflected in such mythic disguises as 'Joan of Arc' and 'The Spanish Military Nun.' Meanwhile, with new-found powers of imagination he devotes himself to a more extensive and externally oriented exploration of the cosmos ruled by the apocalyptic power briefly glimpsed in 'Savannah-la-Mar.' It is a fruitful pursuit, leading as it does to *The English Mail-Coach* of 1849, the chief document in establishing De Quincey's claim to a place among the major English writers in the visionary tradition. *Suspiria de Profundis* remains a heroic attempt, a bold assertion *in propria persona* of De Quincey's worth as an imaginative man, but it founders on the refractoriness of personal experiential detail to the thrust of a visionary consciousness.

⚓[5]⚓

God and Death:
The English Mail-Coach
and Other Writings

I HISTORY, TECHNOLOGY, AND THE SELF

In the seminal vision of *Suspiria de Profundis* a child pursues, through the medium of a trance, the retreating throne of God and is repelled by a 'Sarsar wind of death,' which returns him to his mortal state in a room with a corpse. The preceding chapter has explained these images in terms of the child's subjective development, as befits the dominant theme of the *Suspiria* as a whole. But the presences of God and death preside over De Quincey's most significant imaginative works of the late 1840s, the brief and powerful 'System of the Heavens' (1846) and the extraordinary *English Mail-Coach*, works which transcend purely personal contexts and extend the range of his imagination to technological, historical, and even cosmic concerns. A brief glance again at the *Suspiria* vision from a different perspective may provide us with a skeletal model of the dialectic which informs these works. In this vision the throne of God is conceived as a kind of dynamic vehicle moving ahead of and in the same linear direction as the expanding consciousness of the mortal perceiver gravitating towards it. Death is also conceived as a dynamic force, a 'wind' moving in the opposite direction from the throne and against the perceiver. The unstated but obvious corollary is that the wind of death must emanate from the region of the throne itself. Death and God are thus presented as powers in contrary motion but deriving their energy from the same mysterious point.

This engagement of powers with each other and with the human consciousness provides a model for the structure of De Quincey's beliefs (particularly as they are expressed in his later writings) concerning the operation of forces in the world beyond the self, the world of natural and human history. Although the works to be considered in this chapter eventually bring these beliefs to bear upon the situation of the subjective consciousness, a survey of the beliefs themselves, drawing upon a variety of scattered writings, may best introduce us to these works.

In De Quincey's thought the pursuit of the ever-soaring throne of God finds its expression, on the suprapersonal level, in the accelerating development of technological and historical change towards a self-perfecting ideal, which is both the energizing force and the goal of this acceleration. This is a theory of 'Christianity in the grip of progress,' to use the phrase of E.T. Sehrt, whose German monograph on De Quincey's metahistorical beliefs and their affinities to Hegelian and Kantian traditions remains the best study of the subject.[1] What distinguishes De Quincey's treatment of these ideas, by no means original to him, is the messianic fervour with which he entertains them, the obvious straining of his eyes to descry the apocalypse hovering upon the horizon of historical time. His characteristic mixture of diffidence and fascination before the manifestation of dynamic assertive force sometimes seems to give way, at least on the level of theory, to an enthusiastic commitment to the triumph of this force.

Thus in an undated fragment, published posthumously and obviously late in composition, De Quincey reads the grandeur of Britain's destiny in modern improvements in rail communications:

And thus it is that all the nation, thus, 'all that mighty heart,' through nine hundred miles of space, from Sutherlandshire by London to the myrtle climate of Cornwall, has become and is ever more becoming one infinite harp, swept by the same breeze of sentiment, reverberating the same sympathies
'Here, there, and in all places at one time.'
Time, therefore, that ancient enemy of man and his frail purposes, how potent an ally has it become in combination with great mechanic changes! Many an imperfect hemisphere of thought, action, desire, that could not heretofore unite with its corresponding hemisphere, because separated by ten or fourteen days of suspense, now moves electrically to its integration, hurries to its complement, realizes its orbicular perfection, spherical completion through that simple series of improvements which to man have given the wings and *talaria* of Gods.[2]

Language hitherto reserved for describing the unifying powers of dreams ('integration,' 'complement,' 'orbicular perfection, spherical completion') is now applied to the fruits of mechanical contrivance, and even the great

Romantic exponents of a retreat from mechanism, Wordsworth (quoted twice in this passage) and Coleridge (whose 'Eolian Harp' is clearly commemorated here), are pressed into the same service. Mechanism itself evolves into that which is beyond mechanism, a truly organic form, a 'One Life' that reminds us of the visionary Giant Man that haunts De Quincey's imagination. The development of the telegraph, for example, an even swifter communicator than the railroad, sends him into a virtually prophetic rapture. Thus he asks us, in a passage added in 1853 to an autobiographical sketch written years before, to

conceive a state of communication between the centre and the extremities of a great people, kept up with a uniformity of reciprocation so exquisite, as to imitate the flowing and ebbing of the sea, or the systole and diastole of the human heart ... and then every part of the empire will react upon the whole with the power, life, and effect of immediate conference amongst parties brought face to face. Then first will be seen a political system truly *organic* – i.e., in which each acts upon all, and all react upon each: and a new earth will arise from the indirect agency of this merely physical revolution. Already, in this paragraph, written twenty years ago, a prefiguring instinct spoke within me of some great secret yet to come in the art of distant communication. At present I am content to regard the electric telegraph as the oracular response to that prefiguration. But I still look for some higher and transcendent response.   (I, 270–1)

In this evolution of the mechanical into the organic there lies the seed of an even mightier evolution of the human into the divine. De Quincey's presentiment of 'a new earth' clearly implies its apocalyptic complement of a 'new heaven,' presumably the higher and transcendent response sought for here. The precise nature of such a 'new heaven' remains obscure, but it plausibly involves some sort of emergence of the Godhead not in isolation from human temporality but rather as its consummating climax, like the 'one far-off divine event' of Tennyson's *In Memoriam*. In 'Savannah-la-Mar' De Quincey spoke of God's present as the human future, but there the terminology is surely figurative, and the different planes of being are kept distinct. Although De Quincey never abandons the doctrinally orthodox position that the deity is complete and perfect from the beginning, imaginatively he is, like Tennyson, more ambiguous about this than he knows. It is difficult not to elicit from passages such as those cited above a sense in which the power of the Godhead is coterminous with the entire dynamic thrust of human social, institutional, and technological development when viewed *sub specie aeternitatis.*

The emergence of this power is not accomplished, however, without some prefatory costs. Celebrations of national energies are too frequently accompanied by celebrations of the energies of war. In 'Recollections of Charles Lamb' (1838) De Quincey presents the Battle of Waterloo as a kind of Armageddon, issuing in the millennium and creating out of turmoil a supranational community centripetally organized about England: 'Triumph, however, in the sense of military triumph, was lost and swallowed up in the vast overthrow of evil, and of the evil principle. All nations sympathized with England – with England, as the centre of this great resurrection; centre for the power; centre, most of all, for the moral principle at work' (III, 62). In the essay 'On War' of 1852 De Quincey makes even greater claims: 'The great phenomenon of war it is [he has Waterloo particularly in mind], this and this only, which keeps open in man a spiracle – an organ of respiration – for breathing a transcendent atmosphere' (VIII, 392). 'This and this only': in *Suspiria de Profundis* the organ for communicating with the transcendent was the dream faculty, which could be cultivated only in isolation from the external tide of human affairs, the reverse of his position in 'On War.' Sublimity resides either in a wholly introverted turning to the privacy of the dream experience, or, alternatively, in an impersonal movement of national destiny which subsumes the dreams of individuals and often demands their very life-blood to fulfil its missions.

In choosing the moment of the battle of Waterloo as the crucial point in the triumphant unfolding of British historical destiny De Quincey expresses a possible ambiguity in his attitude towards this triumph. Except for the recording of some dreams in the last part of the *Confessions*, not a single personal experience recalled in his writings occurs after 1815, as if all the later events in his life were dross. As a point of fact Waterloo occurred in the midst of a period (roughly 1813–15) that marked a major transition in De Quincey's life from a youth of relative serenity and security to a maturity filled with anxiety, need, and the pains of addiction. But the development of history, as he reads it, moves in precisely the opposite direction, from the disarray of twenty-five years of strife before Waterloo to a state of coalescence, which knits not only British society together in unity but all of Europe as well. Personal and external history seem to move reciprocally upon counter-cycles, as if the external tends to absorb and renew the lost bliss of the individual, a situation which could account for the urgency of De Quincey's faith in the impersonal dynamic of history and also suggest the poignancy of that faith.

It follows that only a slight shift in focus may convert hymns to universal progress into laments over individual diminishment and pain. The malicious hostility of governments figures significantly in 'The Revolt of the Tartars,' 'The Avenger,' and 'The Household Wreck,' and in the latter work the ongoing motion of society is conceived as a brutal, destructive force: 'The mighty Juggernaut of social life, moving onwards with its everlasting thunders, pauses not for a moment to spare, to pity, to look aside, but rushes forward for ever, impassive as the marble in the quarry, caring not for whom it destroys, for the how many, or for the results direct and indirect, whether many or few' (XII, 159–60). The figure of the Juggernaut is applied specifically here to social change, and De Quincey fastens conspicuously upon the motif of vehicular speed, the same motif that spells glory in the celebrations of national power, as the agency of destructiveness. Later in the 'Introductory Notice' to *Suspiria de Profundis*, a work devoted to proclaiming the imaginative grandeur of a self that develops in solitude, both the beneficent and destructive aspects of technological advance induce in him a profound disturbance:

Already, what by the procession through fifty years of mighty revolutions amongst the kingdoms of the earth, what by the continual development of vast physical agencies, – steam in all its applications, light getting under harness as a slave for man, powers from heaven descending upon education and accelerations of the press, powers from hell (as it might seem, but these also celestial) coming round upon artillery and the forces of destruction, – the eye of the calmest observer is troubled; the brain is haunted as if by some jealousy of ghostly beings moving amongst us; and it becomes too evident that, unless this colossal pace of advance can be retarded (a thing not to be expected), or, which is happily more probable, can be met by counter-forces of corresponding magnitude, – forces in the direction of religion or profound philosophy that shall radiate centrifugally against this storm of life so perilously centripetal towards the vortex of the merely human, – left to itself, the natural tendency of so chaotic a tumult must be to evil; for some minds to lunacy, for others a reagency of fleshly torpor. (XIII, 334–5)

Although there is a hint here of his allegiance to the battle-God of Waterloo (the use of artillery is not infernal but in fact celestial), De Quincey contradicts this half-hearted suggestion by considering all modern technology as tending 'towards the vortex of the merely human' (and the 'merely' is significant). But if technological development is stripped of its transcendent aura, it retains all its more than human attributes of power. It attains personified form in 'ghostly beings,' stalking like De Quincey's giant figures 'with colossal pace'; it moves centripetally (a hallmark of higher power), and the forces of religion and philosophy (though of 'corresponding magnitude') are assigned a garrison status of defending the circumference of their own province against the hosts of the enemy rushing in at all sides.

The stresses of external experience inimical to an introspective consciousness inevitably create feelings of anxiety and personal incapacity. These feelings are the dark companions of all the remarkable productions of imaginative prose that issue from De Quincey's pen in the 1840s. Writing to a friend in 1844, while at work on the *Suspiria*, he despairs of its success:

In parts and fractions eternal creations are carried on, but the nexus is wanting, and life and the central principle which should bind together all the parts at the centre, with all its radiations to the circumference, are wanting. Infinite incoherence, ropes of sand, gloomy incapacity of vital pervasion by some one plastic principle, that is the hideous incubus upon my mind always.[3]

One notices that the incapacities for which he scourges himself are precisely the negatives of those qualities which he attributes to the nation-state in its technological advance: centripetal organization, a network of communication between circumference and centre, a shaping teleology or 'plastic principle' that guarantees forward momentum. If there is any solace to be gained from the prophetic hope that mechanism will attain organic form, it is counterbalanced by a desperate surmise that organic vitality has fled the subjective consciousness itself.

De Quincey's sense of personal failure overspreads his projects 'with a dark frenzy of horror,' he writes to Nancy Mitford in 1846,[4] and in 'Sir William Hamilton' (1852) he gathers the various agents of his pain into the figure of 'some unknown snake-like enemy, in some unknown hostile world, brooding with secret power over the fountains of one's own vitality' (v, 305). This sense of a coalescent evil principle often gives a Manichaean cast to De Quincey's theological speculations. In the essay 'On Christianity' of 1846, the year of his letter to Miss Mitford and of the 'System of the Heavens,' he writes: 'Dark natures there may be whose *essence* is evil, that may have an abiding root in the system of the universe not less awfully exempt from change than the mysterious foundations of God' (VIII, 225). If the God of De Quincey's metaphysics is essentially a principle of gathering unity, whether manifest inwardly as the imagination's Giant Man, outwardly as the dynamic modern state, or abstractly as a personified ruler, the fundamental evil is essentially a principle of universal death, and it is manifest subjectively in the individual's incapacity and objectively in the ruthless destructiveness of organized power. The two principles are not so much static counter-forces as the obverse and reverse of the same reality, mutating into one another according to the spectator's vantage-point. There is ultimately, as De Quincey says in words added to the trance-vision of 'The Affliction of Childhood' in 1853, 'some mighty relation between God and death' that 'evolve[s] itself from the dreadful antagonism between them' (I, 42). This is the dialectic of apocalypse, the movement towards ultimate unification that follows upon the ultimate polarization of antagonist powers. Yet it is disquieting, an apocalypse without victory, for the 'dreadful antagonism' becomes a 'mighty relation,' a union of unspecified strength. At best the power of death comes to support God's purposes; at worst God and death become homologous terms, a fear that goes to the bottom of De Quincey's dark imaginings.

II GOD AND DEATH IN THE COSMOS:
'SYSTEM OF THE HEAVENS'

'System of the Heavens as Revealed by Lord Rosse's Telescopes' (VIII, 7–34), published in 1846, is a powerful though little-known work which offers an imaginative synopsis of the thematic dialectic outlined more generally in the preceding paragraphs. An altogether less ambitious work than *Suspiria de Profundis* of the preceding year, 'System of the Heavens' focuses on a region of De Quincey's imaginative landscape that the *Suspiria* virtually ignores, the domain of horror and destructive power, and it does so by deriving visionary experience from external, quasi-scientific data almost wholly removed from the visionary's personal experience. The essay is ostensibly a review of *Thoughts on some Important Points relating to the System of the World*, by J.P. Nichol, a close personal friend of De Quincey and a popularizer of astronomical topics. What starts as an informal book review concludes as a formal dream-allegory. 'My purpose, 'De Quincey says in a note added at the republication of the piece in 1854, 'was ... from amongst the many relations of astronomy ... to select such as might allow of a solemn and impassioned, or of a gay and playful, treatment. If, through the light torrent *spray* of fanciful images or allusions, the reader catches at intervals momentary glimpses of objects vast and awful in the rear, a much more impressive effect is likely to be obtained' (VIII, 8n). The variation of tone in this work represents a stylistic equivalent to the agility of a mind responding to the ambiguous shiftings of external reality. These shiftings both conceal and advertise the presence of giant forms, polar principles writ large upon the cosmos.

Three passages of heightened imaginative intensity pierce through the more trivial material of the essay to give it its literary significance. The first is a beautiful meditation upon the earth itself as it moves through its cycles of natural history:

Perhaps, in reality, the Earth is both young and old ... In fact, she is a Phoenix that is known to have secret processes for rebuilding herself out of her own ashes. Little doubt there is but she has seen many a birth-day, many a funeral night, and many a morning of resurrection. For, listen: – Where now the mightiest of oceans rolls in pacific beauty, once were anchored continents and boundless forests. Where the south pole now shuts her frozen gates inhospitably against intrusions of flesh, once were probably accumulated the ribs of empires; ... even where little England, in her south-eastern quarter, now devolves so quietly to the sea her sweet pastoral rivulets, – once came roaring down, in pomp of waters, a regal Ganges, that drained some hyperbolical continent, some Quinbus Flestrin of Asiatic proportions, long since gone to the dogs. All things pass away. Generations wax old as does a garment: but eternally God says: – 'Come again, ye children of men.' Wildernesses of fruit, and worlds of flowers, are annually gathered in solitary South America to ancestral graves: yet still the Fauna of Earth, yet still the Flora of Earth, yet still the Sylva of Earth, does not become superannuated, but blossoms in everlasting youth. Not otherwise, by secular periods, known to us geologically as facts, though obscure as durations, *Tellus* herself, the planet, as a whole, is for ever working by golden balances of change and compensation of ruin and restoration. She recasts her glorious habitations in decomposing them; she lies down for death, which perhaps a thousand times she has suffered; she rises for a new birth, which perhaps for the thousandth time has glorified her disc. (VIII, 10–11)

This passage reflects the synoptic vision of nature that runs through the English poetic tradition from Spenser's Garden of Adonis and the 'Mutability Cantos,' through Keats's 'Autumn' and some of the late stanzas of Tennyson's *In Memoriam*, to Wallace Stevens's ever-changing 'theatre in the clouds' in his 'Auroras of Autumn.' In the context of De Quincey's own work the world evoked here belongs to the dream-like pastoral settings of 'The Affliction of Childhood,' and particularly the 'involute' visions of death interfused with summer. Like Elizabeth, tutelary divinity of those visions, the goddess described here is both a beloved and a mother-figure, forever dying and resurrected, a flower gathered to ancestral graves yet 'blossoming in everlasting youth.' Despite God's call to the generations, the passage chiefly celebrates the divinity of natural process itself, the phoenix-like immortality conferred by the eternal return of nature's cycles.

The passage ends, however, on a more theistic note: 'Hers is the wedding-garment, hers is the shroud, that eternally is being woven in the loom of *palingenesis*. And God imposes upon her the awful necessity of working for ever at her own grave, yet of listening for ever to his far-off trumpet of resurrection' (VIII, 11). An increased severity marks these lines, with their emphasis on the grave, on awful necessities, and on God's imposition of labour, and signs of resurrection are no longer woven into the daily process of nature but are 'far-off.' There is a hint of tension between the benevolent and suffering mother-figure and the powerful father, who shall put an end to time and process with the blast of the apocalyptic trumpet. But it remains only a hint; for if the alternation of death and rebirth are to go on 'for ever,' then there will be no end to the temporal continuity of natural process; apocalypse and temporal process are apparently disjunctive terms.

Mediating, however, between the idea of eternal cycle and the idea of apocalypse, time's end, is the notion of teleological progress. De Quincey now inserts this notion to bridge the gap between the familiar planet and the unknown heaven above:

Is it not ... a clear presumption that the great career of earthly nations is but on the point of opening, when the main obstacles to effectual locomotion, and therefore to extensive human intercourse, are first of all beginning to give way? Secondly, I ask peremptorily, Does it stand with good sense, is it reasonable, that Earth is waning, science drooping, man looking downward, precisely in that epoch when, first of all, man's eye is arming itself for looking effectively into the mighty depths of space? A new era for the human intellect, upon a path that lies amongst its most aspiring, is promised, is inaugurated, by Lord Rosse's almost awful telescope. (VIII, 14)

Upon the cyclic process of nature is mounted an arc of linear human progress leading, through effective communication, to a new human community, and, through scientific discovery, to the solution of cosmological mysteries. Progress on earth has brought man, in the guise of the astronomer, to 'the shores of infinity' (VIII, 16), where his vision will transcend earthly limitations. The telescopic tube, revealing the infinities of the heavens, is thus a material analogue of the 'great tube' of the dream faculty described in the *Suspiria*, 'the magnificent apparatus which forces the infinite into the chambers of a human brain, and throws dark reflections from eternities below all life upon the mirrors of that mysterious *camera obscura* – the sleeping mind' (XIII, 335).

As below, so above; if dark reflections emerge from the infinite space of the dream to trouble the individual, there is no reason to suppose that the astronomical explorer of the infinite should not encounter a correlative darkness. This is the risk that attends all similar ventures into the freedom of the infinite in De Quincey's writings. In one of those total reversals of mood characteristic of these writings he presents this theme in the second of the work's major visions. The great nebula of Orion, viewed telescopically, provides the occasion for a remarkable prose fantasia, which seeks to unmask a recurrently appearing enemy power. The nebula is famous, he says,

for the unexampled defiance with which it resisted all approaches from the most potent of former telescopes; famous for its frightful magnitude, and for the frightful depth to which it is sunk in the abysses of the heavenly wilderness; famous just now for the submission with which it has begun to render up its secrets to the all-conquering telescope; and famous in all time coming for the horror of the regal phantasma which it has perfected to eyes of flesh. Had Milton's 'incestuous mother,' with her fleshless son, and with the warrior angel, his father, that led the rebellions of Heaven, been suddenly unmasked by Lord Rosse's instrument, in these dreadful distances before which, simply as expressions of resistance, the mind of man shudders and recoils, there would have been nothing more appalling in the exposure; in fact, it would have been essentially the same exposure: the same expression of power in the detestable phantom, the same rebellion in the attitude, the same pomp of malice in the features towards a universe seasoned for its assault.   (VIII, 17–18)

In this fancied likeness of the telescopic image of the Orion nebula to a death's-head De Quincey finds the ultimate form of the destroyer-figure, the epitome of the demonic murderer in the entranced 'deep recess' of existence in 'The Knocking at the Gate in *Macbeth*,' the 'unknown snake-like enemy, in some unknown hostile world' of 'Sir William Hamilton,' now identified and located. De Quincey's profound imaginative involvement with *Paradise Lost*, centring on the feeling that the chief loss was freedom from the bane of death, makes the Miltonic allusion virtually inevitable here, and he even seems to be suggesting that Milton's mythological figure and the astronomical apparition are to be identified, that the myth has found its scientific verification. In almost every respect the image stands in antithetical contrast to the vision of the earth presented earlier: a cruel male ruler instead of a benevolent and serving mother, fixed and immutable rather than perpetually changing in cyclic process, manifested in a black and remote waste rather than embodied in a fertile pastoral landscape. If the first vision gives us the figure of a lovely female listening for a benevolent God's trumpet of resurrection, the second presents an apocalypse of a contrary sort, revealing a God of destruction: 'his solemn uncovering by astronomy ... is like the reversing of some heavenly doom, like the raising one after another of the seals that had been sealed by the Angel in the Revelation' (VIII, 21). The second climactic swell of the essay thus comes to its end by neatly reversing the tenor of the first, calling into question all of the postulates of a benevolent cosmos suggested earlier.

For much of the remainder of the essay De Quincey retires, as if in recoil from this ghastly image, and devotes his attention to more prosaic astronomical topics. Isolated phrases, however, maintain the note of anxiety: 'the oppression of distance,' stellar images 'tortured into closer compression' (VIII, 22), 'fraudulent stars,' a star drifting 'with no prospect of coming to an anchorage' (VIII, 26). If external space is, as De Quincey conceives, a projection of 'the depths and the heights which are in man' (VIII, 15), then it is easy to see that this anxiety and the optimistic cheer of the early part of the essay represent the poles of De Quincey's own emotional states and not an objective reading of astronomical and geophysical realities. Even the apparition of the death's-head, though located in Orion, has its proper home in the dream-world: 'he is now a vision "to dream of not to tell"': he is ready for the worship of those that are tormented in sleep' (VIII, 21). The place for the resolution of the fierce antithesis which the essay has now evoked is in the dream, and to this region the essay finally makes its way.

The conclusion of 'System of the Heavens' is a precisely labelled 'Dream-vision of the Infinite as it reveals itself in the Chambers of Space'

(VIII, 33). This vision is loosely based upon Jean Paul's 'Traum über das All' (from *Der Komet*), which De Quincey translated in 1823 (see XI, 290–3).[5] In Jean Paul's dream the dreamer is conveyed by a 'Fair Form' through the voids and the stellar formations of the universe, a journey which is at first oppressive. Eventually, however, he witnesses a kind of Gnostic reversal of spirit and matter in which the stars become dark and the voids between them bright, and he is comforted by a final vision of the Madonna and Child. In 'System of the Heavens' De Quincey omits all of this pious consolation, allowing his dreamer no comforts from the world of innocence. Here the dreamer is summoned to the 'vestibule of heaven' in order to see what God calls 'the glory of my house' (VIII, 33). The initial scene of God enthroned, surrounded by his servants, conveys associations of the traditional palace of heaven, but this palace is apparently only the vestibule of the true natural heavens, where an even more elaborate architecture communicates a sense of the dissolution of all traditions, the falling away of all stability:

To the right hand and to the left towered mighty constellations, that by self-repetitions and by answers from afar, that by counter-positions, that by mysterious combinations, built up triumphal gates, whose architraves, whose archways – horizontal, upright – rested, rose – at altitudes, by spans, that seemed ghostly from infinitude. Without measure were the architraves, past number were the archways, beyond memory the gates. Within were stairs that scaled the eternities above, that descended to the eternities below: above was below, below was above, to the man stripped of gravitating body: depth was swallowed up in height insurmountable, height was swallowed up in depth unfathomable.   (VIII, 34)

De Quincey's prose splendidly imitates what it describes; the 'self-repetition' of parallel construction conveys the sense of reduplicating architecture, while the abrupt phrasing and rocking rhythms ('whose architraves, whose archways – horizontal, upright – rested, rose') suggest simultaneously harsh rectangularities and an unending fall to fragmentation and dissolution. De Quincey's insistence on architectural imagery heightens the irony of the vision, for he is describing a 'house' after all, the dwelling for the presumed source of all order, and architecture is the functional derivative of geometrical perfection. But one senses here only the geometry of the delirium dream, of a waste chaos striving fitfully for geometrical form, of geometrical form disintegrating constantly into chaos.

The ironic implications of the whole work are now manifest. In the telescope the observer sees the figure of death; in dreams he sees the throne of God, that God who earlier in the essay was to call earth and her children to resurrection; but the house of God turns out to be indistinguishable from the domain of the death's-head, who is its only suitable tenant. The dreamer finally wearies of his vision and exclaims: 'Insufferable is the glory of God's house. Let me lie down in the grave, that I may find rest from the persecutions of the Infinite; for end, I see, there is none'; to which his guiding angel answers, rather cruelly: 'End is there none to the Universe of God? Lo! also THERE IS NO BEGINNING' (VIII, 34), and with these emphasized words, that cancel out the opening of Genesis, 'System of the Heavens' concludes. We finish with an apocalyptic vision that denies the validity of traditional apocalyptic thought, the concept of the universe developing through time from a fixed beginning to a fixed end, just as the vision with its imagery of fragmented architectural forms obliterates the notion of a soft and warm garment of renewing life woven on the loom of palingenesis.

It is difficult to ascertain De Quincey's intent in presenting a God who cruelly mocks the faith placed in his goodness by the horrors of his creation.[6] In the concluding dream-vision man's attempts to reach for infinity are checked by his discovery of an appalling cosmos that can signify only his diminishment. Just as the genial vision of earth's cycle of death and rebirth perhaps masks and compensates for a dread of nature's unceasing rapacity, for which the death's-head is only a transplanted figuration, so too does De Quincey's pride in human technology exist side by side with an anxiety about human systems and their close alliance with the powers of chaos. 'System of the Heavens' thus captures deep ambiguities in De Quincey's thought concerning the relation of God and death, of human power and human destructiveness, of pastoral repose and nightmare, themes which *The English Mail-Coach* develops even more intensively, resolving in the world of dreams the ironies which that world has here unveiled.

III TOWARDS APOCALYPSE: *THE ENGLISH MAIL-COACH*

The English Mail-Coach, first published in 1849 in *Blackwood's Magazine* and revised slightly for the Collective Edition in 1854, incorporates a remarkably heterogeneous range of styles, levels of seriousness, and topics of concern, and it fashions these materials in contrapuntal arrangements that press towards a final visionary synthesis. As Robert Hopkins astutely observes (in the only full treatment of *The English Mail-Coach* hitherto published), 'the point of view of the "narrator" of the *Mail-Coach* is that of a visionary and reflective thinker whose consciousness expands to discover new connections between continually widening circles of experience.'[7] The progressive manifestation of these circles of concern – mail-coaches, England, war, death, Judgment, apocalypse, each term encompassing the preceding – gives one kind of pattern of organization to a work that might seem at first glance formless. On this pattern De Quincey superimposes a systolic and diastolic variation of focus and emotional intensity, as the line of narrative rebounds alternately between passages of general survey and isolated epiphanic episodes, between experience outwardly perceived and experience recreated in dreams. Finally there is a corresponding pattern of sharply alternating moods, like those in 'System of the Heavens,' in which the consciousness of the narrator is repeatedly lulled, harrowed, and exalted by the subjects of its contemplation. This tri-partite organization of moods not only governs the rendering of particular episodes but, in a general way, is writ large in the work's three major subdivisions, 'The Glory of Motion,' 'The Vision of Sudden Death,' and the 'Dream-Fugue.'

The grand subject of these energetically varied responses is a familiar one that has increasingly pressed its claims over three decades of De Quincey's writing – power in alliance and at odds with the individual consciousness. The mail-coach and its team function as the primary emblem of this power:

1st, through velocity at that time unprecedented – for they first revealed the glory of motion; 2dly, through grand effects for the eye between lamp-light and the darkness upon solitary roads; 3dly, through animal beauty and power so often displayed in the class of horses selected for this mail service; 4thly, through the conscious presence of a central intellect, that, in the midst of vast distances – of storms, of darkness, of danger – overruled all obstacles into one steady co-operation to a national result. For my own feeling, this post-office service spoke as by some mighty orchestra, where a thousand instruments, all disregarding each other, and so far in danger of discord, yet all obedient as slaves to the supreme *baton* of some great leader, terminate in a perfection of harmony like that of heart, brain, and lungs in a healthy organisation. But, finally, that particular element in this whole combination which most impressed myself, and through which it is that to this hour Mr. Palmer's mail-coach system tyrannises over my dreams by terror and terrific beauty, lay in the awful *political* mission which at that time it fulfilled. The mail-coach it was that distributed over the face of the land, like the opening of apocalyptic vials, the heart-shaking news of Trafalgar, of Salamanca, of Vittoria, of Waterloo ... The victories of England in this stupendous contest rose of themselves as natural *Te Deums* to heaven   (XIII, 271–2)

The themes touched upon in this overture to the work are familiar, the messianic conception of national destiny, the treatment of the Napoleonic Wars as a kind of Armageddon, the emergence of the nation-state as an organism through the improvement of mechanism. The whole thrust of De Quincey's metahistorical thought is to bring the prophetic events of biblical revelation from the region of vision and spiritual allegory into historical time and space, to make spiritual events consubstantial with material events. Given this larger transformation, it is inviting to view the coach as a materialization, a technological version, of the thundering, irresistible chariot of the Lord depicted in apocalyptic writings.

These visions of the chariot variously rendered in the Scriptures, in Dante, Milton, Blake, and Shelley, commonly stress the indissoluble unity of the guiding intellect or final cause of the power, the living creatures who are the agencies of the power, and the vehicle itself.[8] De Quincey suggests a similar unity in his vivid descriptions of 'the glory of motion.' The coach combines a technologically advanced design with a traditional interdependence of human and animal power. Hence De Quincey presents the mail-coach as a kind of living creature, the nexus of purpose, intellect, emotion, and organic power, emerging as a single vital principle:

On this system the word was ... ,*vivimus*. Yes, 'magna *vivimus*'; ... we realize our grandeurs in act, and in the very experience of life. The vital experience of the glad animal sensibilities made doubts impossible on the question of our speed; we heard our speed, we saw it, we felt it as a thrilling; and this speed was not the product of blind insensate agencies, that had no sympathy to give, but was incarnated in the fiery eyeballs of the noblest amongst brutes, in his dilated nostril, spasmodic muscles, and thunder-beating hoofs. The sensibility of the horse, uttering itself in the maniac light of his eye, might be the last vibration of such a movement; the glory of Salamanca might be the first. But the intervening links that connected them, that spread the earthquake of battle into the eyeball of the horse, were the heart of man and its electric thrillings – kindling in the rapture of the fiery strife, and then propagating its own tumults by contagious shouts and gestures to the heart of his servant the horse.   (XIII, 283–4)

'We live,' know our speed, our grandeur, through the vitality of the horses; the horses augment their vitality through our patriotic rapture in spreading the news of victory. The 'thrilling' is indeed electric, for an emotional circuitry is suggested in which the muscles of the horses derive their energy almost literally from the energies of battle. National destiny and animal power grasp the human participant in an embrace of nearly erotic intensity.

Throughout this rhapsody there runs, however, a disquieting undercurrent that calls to mind De Quincey's darker meditations on the theme of power. In the background there is 'fiery strife' and the cataclysmic 'earthquake of battle,' and in the foreground 'spasmodic' strength, hoofs that thunder, and eyes that give off a 'maniac light.' These evocations of violence suggest how easily the chariot of glad tidings may become a chariot of wrath, a secularized version of that relentless vehicle of the Messiah in Book VI of *Paradise Lost*, sweeping all before it in its path, not a messenger but an engine of destruction. There is, of course, an element of terror in all apocalyptic imagining, and in the nineteenth century it often becomes associated with mechanistic forces in rapid advance. The most notable example is Shelley's 'Triumph of Life,' where the fourfold chariot of power undergoes a heavily ironic transformation into an agency of universal blight, and elements of the same sort of imagining occur in *Moby Dick*, perhaps under De Quincey's influence.[9] The mail-coach itself demonstrates an alarming tendency to smash into whatever is in its path and to run amuck, despite its participation in a system that is presumably subject to exquisite control. No part of *The English Mail-Coach*, not even the predominantly genial 'Glory of Motion,' escapes this note of anxiety about a power that is feared as much as it is celebrated and is celebrated, it sometimes seems, because it is feared.

The early portion of 'The Glory of Motion' approaches in a gingerly fashion the twin themes of power as attraction and as threat. Both the glory and the terror of the coach are held at a distance, though subtly announced, by a series of anecdotes in the mock-heroic vein. In the first of these a Chinese emperor, presented with a mail-coach by the British government, fails to understand how it is to be guided, and suffers a wild and hair-raising ride (XIII, 276–7). It is difficult to sort out the implications of this anecdote; perhaps it suggests the incapacity of imperial guidance, the wayward powers of its machinery, or, alternatively, the superiority of *British* imperial control. Other anecdotes, set closer to home, contain the same ambiguity. In one episode the young narrator, riding upon the coach, issues whimsical charges of treason against a commercial vehicle attempting to race its royal counterpart (XIII, 281–3); in another episode, more farcical, the relentless course of the mail-coach brings it into collision with a cart full of eggs, with dismaying consequences for the latter, an event the narrator excuses with the remark that 'if even [the coach] seemed to trample on humanity, it did so, I felt, in discharge of its own more peremptory duties' (XIII, 281). The insouciance of these mock-solemn pronouncements derives from the narrator's full self-identification with the coach and its powers: 'We, on our parts (we, the collective, mail, I mean), did our utmost to exalt the idea of our privileges by the insolence with which we wielded them' (XIII, 280). Again, it is difficult to determine which note is dominant in these passages, the sense of insolent power and potential destructiveness or the sense of security, evoked not only by the narrator's station on the coach but also by the enveloping atmosphere of adolescent fun, an atmosphere possible only in a social order that remains essentially benign and stable, for all its broken eggs.

In the remainder of *The English Mail-Coach* the delicate equilibrium presented in these early episodes tends to come apart in proliferating polarizations. The mail-coach goes on to increasingly crucial and fateful engagements, which are, by turns, harrowingly destructive or grandly proclamatory of national salvation. In a corresponding development the consciousness of the narrator, so securely identified with the coach in the early episodes, becomes increasingly focused upon itself and discovers a similar conflict within. The first episode to manifest these trends in a concentrated way seems at the outset to continue the genially humorous tone of the early anecdotes. It involves the coachman's granddaughter Fanny, a lovely and innocently flirtatious girl, who attracts the attentions of Oxford students riding the mail on the Bath Road while her grandfather is engaged in changing the horses. Fanny is another one of De Quincey's female paragons, 'the loveliest young woman for face and person that perhaps in my whole life I have beheld,' and since she dwells 'amongst the lawny thickets of Marlborough forest' (XIII, 285), she is a recognizable embodiment of a familiar topos in his writings, natural innocence located in an appropriately pastoral environment. She is not, however, merely another Elizabeth, for there is a particular emphasis on her sexual attractiveness. She numbers two hundred Oxford men in her train of admirers, and the narrator himself makes 'about as much love' to her 'as one *could* make whilst the mail was changing horses' (XIII, 286). Out of this slight but pleasant situation involving the first innocent quickenings of adult sexual attraction an uncanny terror eventually generates itself in the narrator's consciousness. The coachman, 'a good man ... that loved his beautiful granddaughter, and, loving her wisely, was vigilant over her deportment in any case where young Oxford might happen to be concerned' (XIII, 285), becomes, despite this favourable appraisal of his character, a monstrous figure in De Quincey's dreams.

In the version of 1849 De Quincey's nightmares take the following form:

Out of the darkness, if I happen to call up the image of Fanny from thirty-five years back, arises suddenly a rose in June; or, if I think for an instant of a rose in June, up rises the heavenly face of Fanny ... Then comes a venerable crocodile, in a royal livery of scarlet and gold, or in a coat with sixteen capes; the crocodile is driving four-in-hand from the box of the Bath mail. And suddenly we upon the mail are pulled up by a mighty dial, sculptured with the hours, and with the dreadful legend of TOO LATE. Then all at once we are arrived in Marlborough forest, amongst the lovely households of the roe-deer: these retire into the dewy thickets; the thickets are rich with roses; the roses call up (as ever) the sweet countenance of Fanny, who, being the grand-daughter of a crocodile, awakens a dreadful host of wild semi-legendary animals – griffins, dragons, basilisks, sphinxes – till at length the whole vision of fighting images crowds into one towering armorial shield, a vast embla-zonry of human charities and human loveliness that have perished, but quartered heraldically with unutterable horrors of monstrous and demoniac natures; whilst over all rises, as a surmounting crest, one fair female hand, with the fore-finger pointing, in sweet, sorrowful admonition, upwards to heaven, and having power ... to awaken the pathos that kills, in the very bosom of the horrors that madden, the grief that gnaws at the heart, together with the monstrous creations of darkness that shock the belief, and make dizzy the reason, of man.   (XIII, 290n)

For the first time in the work the mail-coach becomes associated with images of demonic horror and with the defeat of paradisal innocence. Unlike Arden, this is a forest with a clock, a clock more like a tombstone, with a petrified inscription proclaiming some nameless and irrevocable situation. Since the mail-coach relentlessly tries to arrive at its destinations 'on time,' in the process often creating disaster for innocents, the inscription presumably applies to the hapless victims of the coach's onslaught. The associations of national and technological power that constantly attend the image of the coach invite an allegorical reading of this dream situation: perhaps it has become too late for innocence to survive in a world dominated by the onslaught of power, too late to establish a bond of love in the face of 'more peremptory duties' which hustle one off under the watchful eye of stern authority.

Clearly, however, a more profound personal disturbance must lie behind this dream in order to summon up images that 'madden' and 'shock.' While dallying with Fanny behind her grandfather's back the young narrator tended to compare the old man to a crocodile, a resemblance which 'lay in a monstrous inaptitude for turning around' (XIII, 286). Yet the image remains bizarre; why a crocodile and not many other slow and massive beasts more appropriately suggested by a stout old coachman? The first of De Quincey's dream-crocodiles appeared in the climax to 'The Pains of Opium,' where the beast figured as a kind of a monstrous lover to the tortured dreamer, a projection of all his anxieties gathered together. In *The English Mail-Coach* the crocodile becomes associated with the state, since it wears the royal livery, an association strengthened in a digressive passage that precedes the narration of the dream, where De Quincey remarks that 'the Pharaohs and the crocodile domineered over Egyptian society.' and man 'viewed the crocodile as a thing sometimes to worship, but always to run away from' (XIII, 288). The image has now become attached to a significant chain of associations: ancient divine and secular power, English secular authority, the mail-coach, a censorious figure of authority who thwarts love, and yet ultimately a kind of hideous and sinister sexual figure itself. The erotic energy associated with the power of the mail-coach, the sinister Eros of the crocodile in 'The Pains of Opium,' and what we may import to the text from Freud's interpretation of reptilian imagery form an appropriate backdrop to something that the language describing Fanny's afflictions among the monsters with whom she is forced to 'quarter' makes almost explicit. 'Monstrous and demoniac natures,' 'unutterable horror,' 'one fair female hand': these phrases are in the quintessential idiom of nineteenth-century anxiety-fantasies concerning sexuality, and, indeed, why else should the horrors be 'unutterable'? In short the dream links divinely sanctioned authority with repulsive forms, authoritarian repression with active aggression, and poses these against a fragile and tentatively sexual love. As the legendary monsters replace the roses as Fanny's companions, so also does the idea of a possible fruition for innocent love give way to visions of devouring sexuality. Even if the coachman in waking reality is a restraining force, in the dream he becomes a monstrous figure of powerful aggression, for any figure who keeps one from one's love must be at some level a rival for that love.

The grandfather-as-crocodile was originally no threat, however, in waking experience. He became a crocodile, figuratively, through his very incapacity to threaten, that is, to turn around and see what the young lovers were doing. The real potential for aggression lies with the narrator, an impulse that would remain innocent if the presence of the coachman did not charge it with stealth, anxiety, and guilt. Loyalty to a feared power, not the power itself, is the ultimate enemy. Hence the horrific images are ultimately reptiles of the mind, persecutions nominally of the fair beloved but really of the virginal consciousness, the checking of an innocent impulse that comes from within by an impulse of destructive fear also from within, though given loathsome external form by the dream. This point is made explicit in the 1849 version in a lengthy addendum to the vision of Fanny among the monsters, in which De Quincey discusses 'the most terrific [element] that besieges dreams':

viz. the horrid inoculation upon each other of incompatible natures. This horror has always been secretly felt by man; it was felt even under pagan forms of religion, which offered a very feeble, and also a very limited, gamut for giving expression to the human capacities of sublimity or of horror. We read it in the fearful composition of the sphinx. The dragon, again, is the snake inoculated upon the scorpion. The basilisk unites the mysterious malice of the evil eye, unintentional on the part of the unhappy agent, with the intentional venom of some other malignant natures ... But the dream-horror which I speak of is far more frightful. The dreamer finds housed within himself – occupying, as it were, some separate chamber of his brain – holding, perhaps, from that station a secret and detestable commerce with his own heart – some horrid alien nature ... These ... are horrors from the kingdom of anarchy and darkness, which, by their very intensity, challenge the sanctity of concealment, and gloomily retire from exposition. (XIII, 291–2n)

De Quincey omits the passage in the 1854 version of the *Mail-Coach*, thus removing this 'alien nature' still further from exposition, but it goes to the core of the imaginative conflict in the work and is, indeed, one of the central passages in his writings. Here consciousness has only itself for its object and discovers, in its jumbled sense of possessing forces its own and not its own, that the mind is its own envisioned monster, that all loathing is self-loathing. Though these insights retreat, in an anticipatory Freudian fashion, from examination by the consciousness, their momentary revelation here is sufficient to make them the conceptual centre about which revolve those expansive circles of outward concern to which the work now returns in its attention.

Nothing is more characteristic of the narrative development of the *Mail-Coach* than the sudden ascent from the depths that now occurs in the work as it veers away from private to national concerns. The concluding part of 'The Glory of Motion,' subtitled 'Going Down with Victory,' shows the coach in its role as the herald of national victories in the Napoleonic Wars. Universal rapture, a love that unites all social classes and all parts of Britain, attends the progress of the coach, although De Quincey does not fail to recognize the sorrows visited on some by the news of individual casualties in battle. Since this theme of martial celebration is in itself uncomplicated and by now familiar, there is little need to dwell on this section or to supplement the treatment of it in Hopkins's commentary.[10] It is worth pondering, none the less, the extraordinary haste with which the previous nightmares are quite forgotten, as if the narrator were intent upon placating the reigning powers of his imagined world, offering 'Going Down with Victory' as a kind of apology for the heresies of his dream and its subversive glimpse at the monsters of the subconscious. These monsters refuse, however, to stay submerged and burst finally into waking reality in Section II of *The English Mail-Coach*, 'The Vision of Sudden Death.'

The narrative ingredients of this section are simple: the narrator rides beside the dozing coachman in the pre-dawn hours as the coach, lacking control, plunges down the wrong side of the road; a light gig with a pair of lovers in it suddenly appears athwart the path of the coach, and the narrator, unable to wrest the reins from the totally unresponsive coachman, foresees with horror what seems like an inevitable collision fatal to the lovers in their fragile vehicle. All of the motifs of the narrative have appeared before. The imperious forward thrust of the coach towards a smaller vehicle recalls the episode of the egg cart; the coachman, whom De Quincey compares to the statue of an 'imperial rider' or of a 'Charlemagne' (XIII, 313), recalls the Chinese emperor, and like that figure he cannot control the charge of the horses. Moreover, if the coachman encountered earlier resembled a crocodile, this coachman is even more monstrous:

'In fact, he had been foretold by Virgil as
    'Monstrum horrendum, informe, ingens, cui lumen ademptum.'
He answered to the conditions in every one of the items: – 1, a monster he was; 2, dreadful; 3, shapeless; 4, huge; 5, who had lost an eye. (XIII, 306).

Finally, the victims of the monstrous coachman and his engine of destruction, the couple 'tenderly engaged' in a light carriage (XIII, 314), complete a situation which repeats in waking reality the situation represented emblematically in the dreams centring on Fanny. 'The Vision of Sudden Death' thus forms the systolic contraction of the entire work and represents also the eruption into the experiential world of all its motifs except the millennial. Although the experience has all the characteristics of a De Quinceyan dream – the suspenseful confrontation of absolute power and absolute helplessness, the despairing paralysis of the observer – nightmare here becomes waking reality, and the destructive power of the coach is now palpable fact, not a metonymous emblem for other sources of horror.

The whole environmental setting of the episode suggestively duplicates this concentration of the conflict between innocence and destructive power. When the narrator first catches sight of the gig, it is ensconced at the end of an arch of trees resembling the nave of a cathedral (XIII, 314), as if set off in a temple of sanctity which is at the same time a bower of nature. The ambience of the whole scene suggests a dream-like pastoral of innocence, similar to Marlborough Forest, where Fanny dwelt among the roses. But this pastoral setting is located in modern industrial Lancashire, an area suffering under 'the original curse of labour in its heaviest form' (XIII, 310). The theme of ruthless technological advance at war with placid innocence once again plays in the background of the specific episode, and the figure of the slumbering coachman, no longer in control of the horses but still grasping the reins tenaciously, becomes in this context the fit emblem of a nation paradoxically frozen in a course of unbridled power while intellectual control slumbers.[11] The insistence upon the racing of time, the fears that rescue will be 'too late' ('Hurry, then, hurry! for the flying moments – *they* hurry ... Fast are the flying moments, faster are the hoofs of our horses,' XIII, 316) become an expression of the fear of a devouring future and of 'Death the crowned phantom, with all the equipage of his terrors' (XIII, 318) – crowned as the mail-coach (cf 'equipage') is crowned with the insignia of the British government on its side. The Britain proclaimed earlier as the saviour of Christendom is now proclaimed implicitly as the agent of King Death, a fine example of the way that the objects of De Quincey's consciousness tend to reverberate polar associations.

As in the dreams about Fanny, the national drama reflected by the episode is not so important as its reflection of the drama of divided consciousness. The tension in De Quincey's mind between identification with the source of power and horror at its manifestations appears even more vividly in 'The Vision of Sudden Death' than in the episode concerning Fanny, an episode which the 'Vision' recapitulates thematically in ways which are now clear enough. In the earlier episode De Quincey is imaginatively with Fanny against the coachman, but a deeper side of his nature rises up against his conscious desire and releases monsters of anxiety that destroy the image of innocent love. In 'The Vision of Sudden Death' the inner conflict attains expression in an actual physical division: the young lover is a stranger in another carriage, while the narrator rides at the coachman's side. With the coachman asleep, the narrator is in the position of being responsible for control of the coach and yet not responsible, since he is actually as incapable of controlling it as those objectively threatened. As surrogate coachman he is a secure participant in the thrust of power; as sympathetic observer he is terrified and helpless. He thus achieves a simultaneous identification with the destroyer and with the victims. In some remarks prefatory to the narration of the collision incident De Quincey meditates upon this kind of identification:

That dream, so familiar to childhood, of meeting a lion, and, through languishing prostration in hope, and the energies of hope, that constant sequel of lying down before the lion, publishes the secret frailty of human nature – reveals its deep-seated falsehood to itself – records its abysmal treachery. Perhaps not one of us escapes that dream; perhaps, as by some sorrowful doom of man, that dream repeats for every one of us, through every generation, the original temptation in Eden. Every one of us, in this dream, has a bait offered to the infirm places of his own individual will; once again a snare is presented for tempting him into captivity to a luxury of ruin.   (XIII, 304)

This is a radical redefinition of the Fall, for if it traditionally consists in an assertion of individual power against the will of some subordinating force, here it consists in an abnegation of the will before the punitive power of that force. For De Quincey the real Fall, the primal crime against ourselves abiding deeply in our subconscious (below our overt conceptions of sin as forbidden self-gratification), occurs as we cultivate an impotence of the will that invites our ruin, for that ruin is secretly a 'luxury,' our true desire; nemesis and reward are one. Although no overt surrender of the will is involved in the collision episode (the narrator desperately grapples with the coachman's reins and the young man in the gig just as desperately attempts to get his own horse to pull the gig out of the way), the persons involved enact for the reader a *psychomachia* of De Quincey's sense of the Fall: consciousness divided against itself and attaining self-awareness in its sudden external awareness of an approaching destructive principle to which one is elusively but unarguably attached.

These points explain why the most harrowing experience of the whole episode for De Quincey is the moment not of physical impact (as it turns out, the mail-coach does little more than graze the gig) but of the impact on consciousness, specifically that of the terrified girl: 'Oh, heavens! will that spectacle ever depart from my dreams, as she rose and sank upon her seat, sank and rose, threw up her arms wildly to heaven, clutched at some visionary object in the air, fainting, praying, raving, despairing?' (XIII, 317). The vision of sudden death is not in fact the narrator's but the girl's, and it is truly a vision, not an event: 'Suddenly as from the woods and fields – suddenly as from the chambers of the air opening in revelation – suddenly as from the ground yawning at her feet, leaped upon her, with the flashing of cataracts, Death the crowned phantom, with all the equipage of his terrors, and the tiger roar of his voice' (XIII, 318). It is like the Last Judgment, a judgment at which only horror is revealed, but it is also a moment of first revelation, a Fall. The original Fall was traditionally associated with the advent of sexual experience, and death as a ravisher of fair maidens is a commonplace figure in literature. This figure, now associated with the mail-coach itself, which is also crowned with the royal insignia on its sides, brings the sexual undercurrents present throughout the work to their demonic fruition.[12] The girl in the gig experiences not physical death but 'a fate worse,' the death of innocence and innocent love, for dark knowledge becomes lodged in her assaulted consciousness and lodged permanently, as her continued raving and despair (despite the passing of all physical danger) indicate. The narrator shares the same undying vision, coloured even more darkly by an unearned sense of guilt for having helplessly participated in the assault. The tiger-leap of 'Death the crowned phantom' is thus completed not in the temporal event but in the imagination: 'In the twinkling of an eye, our flying horses had carried us to the termination of the umbrageous aisle; at the right angles we wheeled into our former direction; the turn of the road carried the scene out of my eyes in an instant, and swept it into my dreams for ever' (XIII, 318).

The inward thrust which takes horror into the depths of the imagination paradoxically delivers it, however, to a power which is waiting to transform it into the generative matter of an integrated and harmonious vision. The fall into consciousness is accompanied and compensated by a resurrection of the imagination. The product of this imaginative transformation, the 'Dream-Fugue: Founded on the Preceding Theme of Sudden Death,' is perhaps the most energetic apocalyptic vision in English after Blake's 'Night the Ninth' of *The Four Zoas*. Dependent for its power in part upon a non-discursive language of bold images and in part upon a throbbing rhetorical expression, it does not lend itself easily to commentary. None the less the contrary themes developed out of the symbol of the mail-coach – destruction and glory, chaos and control, a disintegrating England and an England renewed – remain clear throughout the sequence of visions. Before these contrary principles attain synthesis in the final vision, the very starkness of the battle must achieve its ultimate power in one last dark involution of visionary experience.

The first vision of the 'Dream-Fugue' opens with a panorama of a tranquil ocean, 'that ancient watery park, within the pathless chase of ocean, where England takes her pleasure as a huntress through winter and summer, from the rising to the setting sun' (XIII, 319). The locale itself provides a notable example of De Quincey's stylized representation of dream processes. The episode described in 'The Vision of Sudden Death' took place in a pastoral spot near the sea. Like the retinal image of a bright colour which lingers after the eyes are closed, the pastoral scene is maintained but in a complementary transposition; we are upon the sea but near the land. The locale thus affords an environmental continuity to the episode on the road near Lancaster, but the transposition gives De Quincey the opportunity to introduce other relevant associations. For unlike the scene described in the 'Vision,' this ocean is anything but silent and unpopulated: 'Ah, what a wilderness of floral beauty was hidden, or was suddenly revealed, upon the tropic islands through which the pinnace moved! And upon her deck what a bevy of human flowers: young women how lovely, young men how noble, that were dancing together ... amidst natural carolling, and the echoes of sweet girlish laughter' (XIII, 319). The two young lovers of the previous experience have evidently multiplied, and expressions of quiet affection have turned into joyous celebrations. The affinities between this scene and the pastoral locale of the collision incident are coloured by a mood recalling the earlier celebrations of national victory. The reference to England as a kind of Diana suggests the mythologized and magical qualities attached to national themes in Renaissance art, and since it appears that the visionary scene, though within England's domain, is located in the tropics, a more modern note of imperial glory is also present. In short, the vision resembles a painting celebrating England's glory in the eary nineteenth century such as might be expected from an artist of mythologizing and idealizing tendencies.

The intrusion at this point of a real English three-decker with 'mighty bows' turns this idyllic scene into something grotesque, as harsh contemporaneity destroys the idealizing effect. The vessel is, of course, a dream-transformation of the English mail-coach, and the pinnace upon which the heroine of the vision and her friends are sailing is the gig athwart the road. With the reappearance of the confrontation the entire environment changes accordingly: 'The revel and the revellers were found no more; the glory of the vintage was dust; and the forests with their beauty were left without a witness upon the seas ... I looked to the weather side, and the summer had departed' (XIII, 319–20). The second vision of the 'Dream-Fugue' exchanges summer for winter, the sea 'tranquil and verdant as a savannah' for the sea in storm. From this point in the work until the final apocalypse the girl's agony repeats itself in an uncontrollable series of identical spasms, while the symbolic environments dance in change as if to illustrate the universality of the catastrophe. The maritime locale of the first vision persists in the second, but it is now revealed for what it is, not an idyllic spot, not an empire of English glory, but a chaos, an abyss, a malicious force desiring to swallow up innocence, its mist and spray forming cathedral arches (XIII, 320) only to mock (as in 'System of the Heavens') the geometry of order and sanctity. Once again the prospect of collision arises, as the angry currents bear the ships towards one another, and once again the two veer at the last moment, leaving for the dreamer only the awful vision of the lady's assaulted consciousness and the devouring mockery of the universe which has been revealed to her:

There she stood, with hair dishevelled, one hand clutched amongst the tackling – rising, sinking, fluttering, trembling, praying; there for leagues I saw her as she stood, raising at intervals one hand to heaven, amidst the fiery crests of the pursuing waves and the raving of the storm; until at last, upon a sound from afar of malicious laughter and mockery, all was hidden for ever in driving showers.   (XIII, 320–1)

In the second vision the dreamer has witnessed the cause of the girl's afflictions but not her ultimate fate, for the mists and storm hide her from further view; in the third, though the cause of the affliction is unknown, the ultimate fate is all too clear. The locale returns to the land, apparently to some barren shore. The dreamer sees the girl run past in terror, her head adorned with a garland of roses 'for some great festival' (XIII, 321), perhaps the oceanic festival lately interrupted, though this scarcely matters. De Quincey dispenses with the apparatus of vehicles and even of monsters as the efficient agents of the catastrophe; the girl meets her fate, despite the dreamer's warning, in quicksand, the devouring vortex of formless matter: 'I saw by the early twilight this fair young head, as it was sinking down to darkness – saw this marble arm, as it rose above her head and her treacherous grave, tossing, faltering, rising, clutching, as at some false deceiving hand stretched out from the clouds – saw this marble arm uttering her dying hope, and then uttering her dying despair' (XIII, 321). The suggestion is not so much that no hand reaches out to save the girl but that such a hand does seem to reach falsely and deceitfully. The girl clutches for the hand of God, but if she receives such a vision, it is of a God who is the most horrid of her mockers. This is the darkest horror which the work attains, and it is precisely at this point that the weeping dreamer hears noises of battle, which suggest either 'the very anarchy of strife, or else ... it is *victory* that is final, victory that swallows up all strife' (XIII, 322). As neatly as the formless abyss of matter swallows up beauty and innocence, the victory of Armageddon swallows up disaster forever, and both events take place simultaneously.[13]

In the temporal world the simultaneous vision of contrary principles both claiming allegiance brings bewilderment and despair to the narrator (which is why the concept of the coach as a dark agent of destruction continually supersedes the concept of it as a harbinger of glory). But in the dream world the principle of simultaneity, of *discordia concors*, is an end in itself, like the technique of counterpoint in the Baroque fugue. The final vision of the 'Dream-Fugue' unites the contrapuntal motifs of national victory and destructive speed. De Quincey is carried away 'in trance' from the scene of the girl's death in the quicksand to 'some distant kingdom' (XIII, 322), away from the dream-kingdom of ultimate destruction to the dream-kingdom of apocalyptic resurrection. There the mail-coach bearing the glorious message '*Waterloo and Recovered Christendom!*' enters the vast dream-cathedral, where tiers of choristers sing in exultation:

Two hours after midnight we approached a mighty Minster. Its gates, which rose to the clouds, were closed. But, when the dreadful word that rode before us reached them with its golden light, silently they moved back upon their hinges ... Headlong was our pace; and at every altar, in the little chapels and oratories to the right hand and left of our course, the lamps, dying or sickening, kindled anew in sympathy with the secret word that was flying past. Forty leagues we might have run in the cathedral, and as yet no strength of morning light had reached us, when before us we saw the aerial galleries of organ and choir. Every pinnacle of the fretwork, every station of advantage amongst the traceries, was crested by white-robed choristers that sang deliverance. (XIII, 322–3)

This cathedral of unearthly magnitude is De Quincey's version of the multi-tiered temple of the heavenly city of prophetic vision, the apocalyptic image as static structure, and a counterpart to the victory chariot, the apocalyptic image as dynamic force. Although this chariot flies once more towards a rendezvous with destruction, the whole building already represents in itself a kind of redemption of destruction images; the vast gates, elsewhere used to suggest the entrance to the abyss, loom as portentously here but form the entrance to the mansion of victory; the forty leagues of little chapels, oratories, aerial galleries, tracery, and fretwork suggest a multiplication of architectural forms beyond grasp, like the ironic 'House of God' in 'System of the Heavens,' but this is the true house, where multiplicity and elaboration attain unity in their reverberations of one song of deliverance. In the design of *The English Mail-Coach* the cathedral is the visual equivalent of a musical chord in which independent and contrapuntal themes unite. It is a synthesis of the nave-like arching of trees where the collision episode took place and of the 'infinite London' thronged with joyous crowds looking down from every window as the coach sped by with news of victory, (XIII, 296). One vast building fuses both the urban and pastoral orders of England, and in so doing transcends both.

In the midst of this architectural synthesis of themes the mail-coach becomes the simultaneous embodiment in motion of two antithetical forces, triumphant joy and destructive power, threatening once again a final figure of sweet innocence blocking its path. After passing a necropolis of England's dead warriors 'from Creci to Trafalgar' the coach encounters

a female child, that rode in a carriage as frail as flowers. The mists which were before her hid the fawns that drew her, but could not hide the shells and tropic flowers with which she played – but could not hide the lovely smiles by which she uttered her trust in the mighty cathedral, and in the cherubim that looked down upon her from the mighty shafts of its pillars. Face to face she was meeting us; face to face she rode, as if danger there were none. 'Oh, baby!' I exclaimed, 'shalt thou be the ransom for Waterloo? Must we, that carry tidings of great joy to every people, be messengers of ruin to thee!' (XIII, 324)

At this point the work grapples directly with the problematic nature of power. The coach bears with it not only its own weight of power but the full weight of triumphant national destiny; the victim is not a young woman, sexually mature and conscious of danger, but a child, surrounded by flowers and fawns, innocent of all consciousness of harm. The profound question, 'shalt thou be the ransom for Waterloo?' suggests the issues involved. By a strange sort of logic it seems that, if the victory of Waterloo is to occur, if a dynamic Christendom is to emerge, pure innocence and pure nature must be sacrificed. It is not the sacrifice of the soldier, who works consciously for the victory, nor even that of the martyr who willingly goes to his fate as an exemplary model, but a transaction in which the victim is entirely passive. It is as if a dark principle of destruction must be satisfied and placated in order for its power to be converted from darkness to constructive use.

But the sympathies of the dreamer rebel in horror at the thought of such a dualistic principle pervading the cosmos, and even those who died for England's good find the notion unendurable: 'Also, in horror at the thought, rose one that was sculptured on a bas-relief – a Dying Trumpeter. Solemnly from the field of battle he rose to his feet; and, unslinging his stony trumpet, carried it, in his dying anguish, to his stony lips – sounding once, and yet once again; proclamation that, in *thy* ears, oh baby! spoke from the battlements of death' (XIII, 324–5). The sound of the trumpet brings a sudden silence and stasis to the whole vast scene, clearly recalling the silence in heaven at the opening of the seventh seal in the Book of Revelation. The sound brings consciousness of death to the little child, and as 'The Vision of Sudden Death' has shown, it is in the moment of conscious apprehension of dark possibilities subsisting within light and peace that the apocalypse takes place. In the frozen moment consciousness comes and innocence disappears, for at the third sounding of the trumpet, when 'the seals were taken off all pulses' (XIII, 325) so that music and motion renew, the child is transformed back into the terrified grown woman of the visions of afflictions – only the fully adult consciousness can recognize destructive potentialities. At this point a new figure enters, a 'better angel' who pleads with heaven for the woman's salvation and finally wins it by his intercession. Whatever this 'better angel' may represent (he may be derived from the young man in the gig whose efforts remove it just in time from the path of the mail-coach), he clearly expresses a mighty wish that the pattern will not take so horrid a form, that the last fruit of consciousness will not be a vision of sudden and triumphant death. In the imagination wish becomes fact, and the girl is saved, but not, significantly, until she has undergone an expansion of consciousness which enables her to conceive her negation at the moment of her salvation.

Once the girl is saved, there is an eruption of final joy and universal resurrection:

Then was completed the passion of the mighty fugue. The golden tubes of the organ, which as yet had but muttered at intervals – gleaming amongst clouds and surges of incense – threw up, as from fountains unfathomable, columns of heart-shattering music. Choir and anti-choir were filling fast with unknown voices ... Pomps of life, that, from the burials of centuries, rose again to the voice of perfect joy, did ye indeed mingle with the festivals of Death? Lo! as I looked back for seventy leagues through the mighty cathedral, I saw the quick and the dead that sang together to God, together that sang to the generations of man. All the hosts of jubilation, like armies that ride in pursuit, moved with one step ... As brothers we moved together; to the dawn that advanced, to the stars that fled; rendering thanks to God in the highest – that, having hid His face through one generation behind thick clouds of War, once again was ascending, from the Campo Santo of Waterloo was ascending, in the visions of Peace; rendering thanks for thee, young girl! whom having overshadowed with His ineffable passion of death, suddenly did God relent, suffered thy angel to turn aside His arm, and even to thee, sister unknown! shown to me for a moment only to be hidden for ever, found an occasion to glorify His goodness. (XIII, 326)

The rhetorical extravagance of this passage, perhaps too florid if judged in isolation, is fully earned here by the mounting intensity of all that has gone before, for this flood of cadenced prose enacts the emotional exuberance of the dreamer at the sudden release from the anxieties of death's power. The resurrection of the dead and the increase in the power of the music, reminiscent of the church scenes in the *Suspiria*, signal that the joy of the apocalypse has at last succeeded its terrors. Resurrection occurs not at the moment when the coach passes through the necropolis with news of victory (that moment stirs only 'earthly passions' and 'warrior instincts' among the dead, XIII, 324) but only when the girl is saved. This suggests that the apocalypse does not inhere in the national victory, but in what the national victory cannot promise, the rescue of individual innocence from the ravages of the experiential world. At the moment when the ideal is fulfilled in one instance, it is fulfilled in all, and the horrid concomitance of national glory and individual disaster disappears.

There is more in this final release of joy than the desperate force of wish-fulfilment, for no darkness contemplated in the course of this work is really excluded in the final vision; rather, it is assimilated in the figure of a destroying and recreating God, who emerges at last, as in the 'Finale' of *Suspiria de Profundis*, as the true protagonist of the work. There is much to make one uneasy in this latest display of De Quincey's God, the God of the mocking visions of infinity in 'System of the Heavens' and of cataclysm in 'Savannah-la-Mar.' Here he is a God neither of mercy nor of wrath, for both attributes depend upon a standard of justice that is wholly absent from the contemplations of power in *The English Mail-Coach*. In this apocalyptic vision we see no casting out of the unrighteous, no struggle against Antichrist, either in the form of the Napoleonic forces (a role easily available to them, so prominent is Waterloo as a *leit-motif* in the work) or in the form of 'Death the crowned phantom,' for the latter figure, as becomes increasingly obvious, is an intrinsic manifestation of God's will. The only victims are figures of unoffending innocence, and their escape depends upon a figure of power who 'relents,' who 'suffers' a persuasion 'to turn aside His arm,' and then finds in this act 'an occasion to glorify His goodness,' behaviour that would be insufferable if judged in human terms.

These considerations, however, give too ironic and antinomian a cast to De Quincey's theological viewpoint in the *Mail-Coach*, for his teleological vision in the work is really not Christian at all, but aesthetic. Nowhere in the work is there any doctrinally orthodox sense of sin or of grace, of the efficacy of faith or of works. The Fall consists not in proud self-assertion but, as the dream of the lion shows, in passive acquiescence to destructive power, and the trials which God visits upon the innocent are designed apparently not to strengthen their moral resistance in a fallen world but to engrave such a world upon their imaginations, to expand their conscious apprehension of a pattern composed of multiple contradictions. Innocence cannot rise to apocalyptic consummation unless it is visited by the principle of destruction and assimilates the principle into itself, and the glory of England shines more gloriously if it is set against the background of the latent destructiveness in national power.[14] God's task is so to intensify human sensitivity to the contradictions of history and of personal experience that they are heard as a kind of fugal music. Hence the 'relenting' that occurs at the end of the

'Dream-Fugue' is not the arbitrary act of some irrascible power but rather an inevitable relaxation of a pressure which it was God's design to apply in the first place, the necessary diastolic response to an act of systolic concentration. In this desire for symmetry in an unfolding pattern we find the reason for the strange progression of the 'Dream-Fugue,' with its deep descent into darkness and its corresponding ascent into light:

A thousand times in the worlds of sleep have [I] seen thee followed by God's angel through storms, through desert seas, through the darkness of quicksands, through dreams and the dreadful revelations that are in dreams; only that at the last, with one sling of His victorious arm, He might snatch thee back from ruin, and might embazon in thy deliverance the endless resurrections of His love! (XIII, 326–7)

The visions of horror have not actually shown 'God's angel' following along, but if he was indeed present, he must have been present in the imaginative principle which demands the attainment of the final tonic chord to conclude the contrapuntal fugue.[15]

The real music of 'Dream-Fugue,' the music that we as readers actually apprehend, is of course not God's but De Quincey's own. It is he who gives the section its title, as well as a notation of tempo for his prose orchestra, *'Tumultuosissimamente'* (XIII, 318), and he weaves his complex texture of *leit-motifs* in a manner that precisely imitates the techniques of Baroque contrapuntal composition.[16] This self-advertising of the work's design points towards the true locus of De Quincey's interest, the artist's consummate powers of ordering the disparates of experience. Like the dream-visions in the *Suspiria*, also heralded by musical metaphors, the ultimate significance of the *Mail-Coach* is inseparable from its form, for the form testifies to the intrinsic power of the otherwise vulnerable man, a power perpetually sought in the awesome Other so that it might be appropriated to the self. Throughout the *Mail-Coach* the power of consciousness rises where the power of an external absolute leaves off. That external power perpetually thrusts upon a passive and initially helpless consciousness a seemingly fatal yet saving knowledge of the dialectic of order and destruction. The dream-faculty then converts this knowledge into a facsimile of God's divine consciousness. The dream however is perishable and needs the music of the prose-poet to arrest it and convert it into the permanently available substance of literary art. Good and evil, God and death, history and personal desire, the divisions of consciousness itself, however endowed in the work with intrinsic interest, finally exist, one comes to believe, for the sake of their counterbalancing parts in a display of integrating art.

It is perhaps too harsh to call this display of integration a totalitarian art-form to match a philosophically totalitarian vision of life, but there is something decidedly chilling in De Quincey's absorption of pain and death as contrapuntal notes in an artfully composed fugue, in his preference, finally, for order in any form at the expense of what is certainly a genuinely felt outrage at the brutalities of experience. Nevertheless he confronts these brutalities – indeed, he insists on confronting them precisely in those areas where his overtly maintained religious and political beliefs would seem to demand a contrary response. Although the objective vision of *The English Mail-Coach* is ethically equivocal and ominously absolutist in its implications, De Quincey's unflinching examination of the sources of anxiety in all its various shapes – historical, social, and personal – remains permanently valuable. The amazing formal intricacy of the work (much of it left unexamined in this commentary) is a testament, moreover, to an attained mastery of the artist's will over the incapacities which anxiety engenders. As a *tour de force* the *Mail-Coach* is unsurpassed in De Quincey's writings; he will not attempt again such imaginative integrations. But here at least, after three decades of seeking, he holds (however obliquely and, one can infer, desperately) the powers of God and Death in his grasp.

❧[6]❧

Last Visions and Revisions

The last decade of De Quincey's life brought him the opportunity to consolidate his literary achievement of the previous thirty years. In 1852, at the invitation of the Edinburgh publisher James Hogg, he began preparation for a collected edition of his writings, an enterprise that was to occupy him until his death in 1859. Not content merely to collect and arrange his various works, De Quincey treated the edition as an opportunity to make revisions of and additions to the established corpus, sometimes minor and sometimes extensive and crucially significant. The more significant revisions include the virtual suppression of *Suspiria de Profundis* and the production of three major new works built out of old ones, the 'Postscript' to 'Murder Considered as One of the Fine Arts' (1854), the *Autobiographic Sketches* (1853), and the second version of the *Confessions of an English Opium-Eater* (1856). This chapter will deal substantially only with the latter two works, but all three provide reassessments of the earlier material out of which they originate.

De Quincey's writing in the 1850s shows no loss of power and effectiveness, a point splendidly corroborated by the expanded *Confessions* produced in his seventy-first year, and he does not abandon the themes which preoccupied him earlier. There are, however, certain telling shifts in sensibility. The myth-making and visionary modes of the 1840s, for example, give way to an emphasis on outward experience, in which preoccupations with self-exploration (as in the *Suspiria*) and fantasized external confrontation (as in 'Murder as One of the Fine Arts') appear in a straightforwardly rendered, dense texture of naturalistic details, and not in the unearthly light of dream-vision.[1] Episodes of euphoria or anxiety become less subject to aggrandizement as myth, and there is less tendency to press contraries, still strongly sensed, into a final imaginative resolution. The major literary enterprise of the aged De Quincey seems to be a retrospective meditation upon the vicissitudes of his experiential journey.

I AUTOBIOGRAPHY REORGANIZED

The first volume of the Collective Edition, *Autobiographic Sketches*, published in 1853, is composed of pieces written for various journals at widely scattered intervals, carefully edited and arranged to form a narrative continuum. This composite autobiography is most notable for its opening piece, none other than 'The Affliction of Childhood,' only slightly altered from the version published as part of *Suspiria de Profundis* in 1845, but now severed from its rich train of allegorical dream-visions. This transplanting indicates that De Quincey has at last abandoned the grand design of the *Suspiria*, the myth of the self-sufficing artist scooping out of existential loss the ore of imaginative vision, for the visions themselves, Levana and her minatory troupe, the azure paradises of the deep, are gone. Something quite different now follows the 'Affliction,' a new piece, written in 1851–2, called 'Introduction to the World of Strife.' This piece brings into prominence De Quincey's domineering elder brother William, a figure whose existence one could not have suspected from the *Suspiria*, where the passing of Elizabeth leads only to a solitude filled with dreams. The addition of a powerful masculine figure to De Quincey's constellation of sibling-guides gives an entirely new context to 'The Affliction of Childhood,' a context that is perhaps meant to be corrective of his earlier design. The great visionary trance in his sister's chamber and the subsequent visions in church now stand in forlorn isolation, followed no longer by triumphs of the imagination but by the child's Babylonian captivity in a typical boyhood world of strife, in which his aggressive brother reigns. A new fidelity to reality is manifest, for the loss of the vision of innocence no longer leads to imaginative compensation but merely to the world of experience.

William is a juvenile version of the omnipotent male force that appears so frequently in De Quincey's writings; he is by turns an inventor, a philosopher, a dramatist, a cruel sultan, a conqueror both in battles with real children in the neighbourhood and in the wars of his imaginary play-kingdom of Tigrosylvania against his brother Thomas's feeble domain of Gombroon (see I, 88 ff). In response to these roles Thomas plays the part of fool, humble subordinate, passive victim, and pariah, and we immediately sense that the 'World of Strife' is a projection into a childhood context of De Quincey's lifelong imaginative responses to the irresistible manifestations of power. But the context itself helps to purge some of the anxiety arising from this manifestation at the same time as it serves as its vehicle. De Quincey narrates William's exploits with a felicitous charm and humour that betray what is essentially a nostalgia for childhood days and a residual affection for this boyish tyrant, the 'King of Tigrosylvania, scourge of Gombroon' (I, 114). One incident concerning these two rival kingdoms suffices to illustrate the finely poised quality of De Quincey's prose in this work. Both boys attempt at first to conceal the precise locations of their kingdoms, Thomas for reasons of fear, William for reasons of guile:

At length, for some reason unknown to me, and much to my astonishment, he located his capital city in the high latitude of 65 deg. north. That fact being once published and settled, instantly I smacked my little kingdom of Gombroon down into the tropics, 10 deg., I think, south of the line ... But my brother stunned me by explaining that, although his capital lay in lat. 65 deg. N., not the less his dominions swept southwards through a matter of 80 or 90 deg.; and, as to the Tropic of Capricorn, much of it was his own private property. I was aghast at hearing *that*. It seemed that vast horns and promontories ran down from all parts of his dominions toward any country whatsoever, in either hemisphere – empire, or republic; monarchy, polyarchy, or anarchy – that he might have reasons for assaulting. (I, 89)

We read the passage ambivalently, detecting either dire manifestations of omnipotent power or the brazen insouciance of boyhood, either the anarchy of nightmare or the arbitrary freedom of children's play. There is an element of the anxiety-dream here in the sudden emotional shocks (Thomas is by turns astonished, stunned, and aghast) and in the huddled climax where sinister peninsulas multiply and virtually come alive to devour similarly multiplied kingdoms. Yet there is a sense of delight, tinged with nostalgia, in this portrayal of the freedom of boys to locate kingdoms and capitals so arbitrarily and so easily, a sense communicated by the jocular bravura of the tone ('instantly I smacked my little kingdom down,' 'as to the Tropic of Capricorn, much of it was his own private property'). De Quincey manages here and elsewhere in the 'World of Strife' to intimate the onset of a period of anxiety and harsh experience and yet to resist the tendency to aggrandize it, as though one viewed this period simultaneously through the eyes of a terrified child and those of a genially nostalgic elderly man. Each perspective stabilizes and gives edge to the other, and each undermines the myth-making tendencies of 'The Affliction of Childhood' in its own way. If the 'world of strife' is a step towards an experiential gloom in which the early pastoral world associated with Elizabeth will seem illusory, it is also a world of imagination in dwindled form; mystic raptures and flights towards God are displaced by the less singular though genuine imaginings of childhood games.

William himself dies at the age of sixteen, and with the passing of this second imaginative guide, so unlike the first, the 'world of strife' also ends, but the course of De Quincey's autobiography takes him towards a further fading of imaginative vision into the light of common day. The next chapter, 'Infant Literature,' deals with nursery reading in a manner resembling Book V of *The Prelude*, and its subject represents another dwindling of imaginative activity from its original manifestation as a visionary grandeur located in the self. To fill out the remainder of *Autobiographic Sketches* De Quincey draws chiefly upon pieces contributed to *Tait's Magazine* in the 1830s, and although some of these are impressively written, particularly the very Wordsworthian description of his first boyhood visit to London (see I, 178 ff), they contain no myth of the inner life, no episodes in the growth of an imagination. Instead, there unfolds fitfully the history of a rich English boy moving among young lords and ladies, a thoroughly minor form of memoir, filled with frequent and often lengthy digressions that have no autobiographical relevance. De Quincey himself points out the centrifugal movement of his narrative and the slackening pressure of his imaginative concerns. His volume, he says, is 'confessedly rambling, and [its] very duty lies in the pleasant paths of vagrancy. Pretending only to amuse my reader, ... I enjoy a privilege of neglecting harsher logic, and connecting the separate sections of these sketches, not by ropes and cables, but by threads or aerial gossamer' (I, 316). Few of De Quincey's writings are notable for 'harsh logic,' if what that phrase means is a keeping to the announced point for any great consecutive length. None the less the distance of the aim stated here from the ambitions at least implicit in *Suspiria de Profundis* is striking. One is tempted to believe that the retrospective imagination of 1853 has lost the ability or the desire to discover a pattern of momentous significance in the cumulative record of personal experience.[2] De Quincey's one splendid endowment, his visionary capacity, now appears to belong only to a receding and finally remote period of early childhood sensibility.

Autobiographic Sketches, a kind of anthology of his previous autobiographical writings, significantly omits what De Quincey calls 'that episode, or impassioned parenthesis, in my life which is comprehended in

"The Confessions of an English Opium-Eater"' (I, 400). It is easy to understand the external reasons why he or his publishers would wish to reserve this most prestigious of his works for a separate place in the edition. Yet the omission, for whatever reason, gives to the *Sketches* an intrinsic design which the inclusion of the momentous London experience and its consequences would have destroyed. In the *Confessions* De Quincey offers a work compact in its narrative, oriented upon the inner life in its climax, and specific in its focus upon the pre-eminent external influence in his life, his addiction. By contrast *Autobiographic Sketches* is loose in construction, increasingly concerned with external events of only superficial interest, and quite devoid of any climax at all, the sketches trailing off inconsequentially as the youth is about to enter Oxford. The autobiography as a whole seems to comprise a process of demythologizing personal history, of acknowledging the inescapable dominance of the light of common day even in the lives of haunted visionaries. Yet perhaps this impression betokens just another De Quinceyan mask, another version of the self created in his continuing search for the essential nature of his past experience. In this latest version the stress falls upon the open-endedness of that experience, its gathering inconsequence, perceived not at all gloomily, yet perceived. That this is a highly selective and truncated version of self-history must be obvious. De Quincey's first autobiographical work, written thirty years before, was also open-ended in its conclusions, yet its emphasis on the ruling alternatives of visionary joy and visionary pain made it far more profoundly revealing of the problematic nature of his experience than anything to be found in the late *omnium gatherum* of *Autobiographic Sketches*. It is aesthetically satisfying that his last major literary effort should involve a return to the *Confessions*, an effort of narrative expansion which restores the theme of imaginative power to its true place of importance in his consciousness while preserving his late respect for experiential detail. A final, extensive commentary is required to do justice to a work which constitutes De Quincey's own most searching commentary on his imaginative life.

II THE REVISED *CONFESSIONS*

1 *Patterns of imagery and theme*

The second version of the *Confessions of an English Opium-Eater* is nearly three times as long as the first. The reason for the expansion, that the work might occupy a volume of comparable length to the others in the collected edition, was fortuitous, but its literary consequences proved deeply rewarding. The most significant expansions occur chiefly in the early portion of the original narrative, before the young hero's experiences in London. Thus the old school, the decision to flee from it, and the course of the flight itself all acquire the vivid colours of detailed treatment. This treatment supplies to the *Confessions* two crucial elements left undeveloped in the first version, a complex psychological motivation and a coherent narrative structure, based on the familiar literary pattern of the epic journey. What was originally a glowing but impressionistic mood piece, glimpsing at states of communal innocence and solitary imaginings, becomes a penetrating autobiographical exploration. The late additions, moreover, cast the incidents retained from the first version in a new light. Now appearing as the cumulative episodes in an experiential journey, they receive new significance from the extended record of experience that precedes them. The new material becomes a kind of commentary on the old, revealing in images created thirty-five years before dimensions of meaning always present and yet latent in their original context.

Critics who have written about the *Confessions* have generally tended to favour the version of 1822, discontented with the lengthy autobiographical prologue later supplied.[3] De Quincey's own attitude in this matter is instructive and reveals his clear awareness of the strength of the later version as a work of self-analysis. Writing to his daughter Emily in 1856 he expresses doubt as to whether the revised version is 'a book to *impress*,' but he also stresses its coherence and studied art: 'Here again ... is a call for choice – between an almost *extempore* effort, having the faults, the carelessness, possibly the graces, of a fugitive inspiration [he refers to the earlier version] – this on the one side, and on the other a studied and mature presentation of the same thoughts, facts, and feelings, but without the same benefit of extempore excitement.'[4] 'A studied and mature presentation' precisely summarizes the essence of the second version of the *Confessions*; it is a more rounded achievement than any of his previous works, more studied than the *Suspiria* in its welding of autobiographical narrative and vision, more mature in its avoidance of strenuous apocalyptic resolutions than *The English Mail-Coach*. The maturity of the late *Confessions* establishes itself not in declarative wisdom, discursively embodied, but implicitly in a rich texture of narrative patterning, recurrent thematic motifs, and symbolic incidents, all mutually reinforcing, a texture which adverse critics have perhaps overlooked. A brief survey of these strategies of expression will help to make the literary structure of the work plain and prepare the way for a more consecutive commentary on its individual parts.

Sequential patterning: the vicissitudes of the journey. The *Confessions* is not really an autobiography in the literal sense of the term, not a complete, chronologically well-proportioned life's history, but rather a condensed or emblematic representation of that history. Its main narrative in the later version describes a journey through three contrasting regions of Britain, and the succession of regions roughly parallels the succession of seasons in a single year. De Quincey returns here to the kind of pattern which informed 'The Revolt of the Tartars' and 'The Spanish Military Nun,' earlier works also dealing with bondage and flight, in which the contrasting landscapes of the journey become expressive of the self-divided consciousnesses of the protagonists.[5] In the *Confessions* this division is manifest in two thematic counter-movements which run through the book concurrently, a downward movement that takes the hero from order and innocence to chaos and suffering and an upward movement that takes him from bondage to physical and imaginative freedom. Both of these themes derive from the same set of autobiographical data: De Quincey's rebellious flight from the Manchester Grammar Schoool, his happy wandering in Wales, his dismal wandering in London, his addiction to opium with its attendant pleasures and pains. De Quincey's adventures in Wales, where he drifts like a creature of nature in accord with 'the eternal motion of winds and rivers' (III, 329), form an existential projection of that thematic stress on the liberation of spontaneous and innocent energies from bondage; his sufferings amid 'the raving, the everlasting uproar, of [the] dreadful metropolis' (III, 344) are a projection of that counter-stress on the dark consequences of rebellion against order. Just as the contrary implications derived from the act of flight present themselves to the journeying boy in the experiential alternatives of pastoral and city, they also present themselves to the experienced adult in the visionary alternatives of heaven and hell, the pleasures and the pains of opium.

Of the two counter-movements, the one towards suffering, towards loss of protected innocence and bondage to experience, receives, on the surface of the book at least, greater stress. After each of the young De Quincey's attempts to escape bondage and suffering there follows a brief period of joy only to be superseded by greater pain. His journey takes him from Manchester, the city of confining restriction, to Wales, the landscape of pastoral freedom, only to return him to a larger city where there are no restrictions and no supports against external suffering and inner desolation. The Manchester Grammar School with its 'dreary expanse of whitewashed walls,' 'gloomy and unfurnished little rooms,' and crypt-like cellars (III, 247, 258, 253), bleak, unimaginative, yet orderly and secure, gives way to buildings emblematic of the countryside, hospitable cottages and wayside inns which combine 'the peace of monasteries ... with the large liberty of nature' (III, 329). These give way in turn to the typical dwelling of the outcast in London, of which Brunell's house, with its 'echoing loneliness' and its 'unhappy countenance of gloom and unsocial fretfulness' (III, 355, 350), is representative. The exuberant imagery of the countryside, 'the eternal motion of winds and rivers,' mutates into the imagery of storm and torrent, the 'everlasting uproar' of urban chaos, and the succession of the seasons during which the main action occurs, from late spring into mid-winter, also corresponds to the downward thematic movement. A new kind of bondage having established itself during the London experience, De Quincey seeks relief once more in the countryside and in the imaginative pleasures of opium. But opium too becomes a bondage, replacing visions of 'halcyon calm' (III, 395) with nightmare visions of formlessness or, alternatively, of ultimate confinement in 'stone coffins' and in 'narrow chambers at the heart of eternal pyramids' (III, 443).

Moments of equilibrium. To mark the transition from states of bliss to states of pain, there are certain pivotal scenes in the narrative in which the sequential movement from one state to the next seems arrested, so that both states appear simultaneously present in a kind of fragile equilibrium. These scenes, in which time becomes slowed to a stasis at once beautiful and ominous, closely resemble the 'involute' passages of the *Suspiria*, where the ideas of death and summer are interfused, where the ominous receives a glow of beauty from its mingling with images of harmony, and harmony seems threatened by a darkness suspensefully postponed yet inevitable. The scenes are strangely dream-like, ceremonial, distanced from the ongoing activities of life. The first occurs at the vesper service read on the last evening De Quincey is to spend at school, a scene in which the long hours of summer twilight become associated with the repose of an ordered little Christian community, and his impending flight with the darkness encroaching upon that haven of repose:

The secret sense of a farewell or testamentary act I carried along with me into every word or deed of this memorable day. Agent or patient, singly or one of a crowd, I heard for ever some sullen echo of valediction in every change, casual or periodic, that varied the revolving hours from morning to night. Most of all I felt this valedictory sound as a pathetic appeal when the closing hour of five P.M. brought with it the solemn evening service of the English Church – read by Mr. Lawson; read now, as always, under a reverential stillness of the entire school. Already in itself, without the solemnity of prayers, the decaying light of the dying day suggests a mood of pensive and sympathetic sadness. And, if the changes in the light are less impressively made known so early as five o'clock in the depth of summer-tide, not the less we are sensible of being as near to the hours of repose, and to the secret dangers of the night, as if the season were mid-winter.   (III, 289–90)

In his prayer 'Lighten our darkness, we beseech thee, O Lord!' were the darkness and the great shadows of night made symbolically significant: these great powers, Night and Darkness, that belong to aboriginal Chaos, were made representative of the perils that continually menace poor afflicted human nature. With deepest sympathy I accompanied the prayer against the perils of darkness – perils that I seemed to see, in the ambush of midnight solitude, brooding around the beds of sleeping nations; perils from even worse forms of darkness shrouded within the recesses of blind human hearts; perils from temptations weaving unseen snares for our footing; perils from the limitations of our own misleading knowledge.   (III, 292–3)

There is a reminiscence of *Paradise Lost* in these passages, not only in the fairly explicit reference to 'Night' and 'aboriginal Chaos,' but also in the stress on valediction and in the references to 'the ambush of midnight solitude' (suggesting Satan's first temptation of Eve), to 'temptations weaving unseen snares,' and to 'misleading knowledge.' For that side of De Quincey's nature which adheres to the principle of order the school appears not as a gloomy house of bondage but as an evanescent garden of innocence. From such a point of view the flight from order constitutes in itself the expulsion from the garden.

The second scene of this sort occurs on De Quincey's last day in Wales, the last day also of a beautiful and lingering Indian summer, and once again in the very lingering of beauty there comes an admonitory sense of impending horror:

It was a day belonging to a brief and pathetic season of farewell summer resurrection, which, under one name or other, is known almost everywhere ... It is that last brief resurrection of summer in its most brilliant memorials, a resurrection that has no root in the past nor steady hold upon the future, like the lambent and fitful gleams from an expiring lamp ... So sweet, so ghostly, in its soft, golden smiles, silent as a dream, and quiet as the dying trance of a saint, faded through all its stages this departing day, along the whole length of which I bade farewell for many a year to Wales, and farewell to summer. In the very aspect and the sepulchral stillness of the motionless day, as solemnly it wore away through morning, noontide, afternoon, to meet the darkness that was hurrying to swallow up its beauty, I had a fantastic feeling as though I read the very language of resignation when bending before some irresistible agency. (III, 343–4)

Despite the reference to hurrying darkness the passage manages to suggest a beauty passing so slowly as not to be passing at all. The stasis of the scene simultaneously contains a prolepsis of death and a protraction of life in the face of impending dissolution. By night dissolution has arrived in the form of a raging storm, which, as the youth watches it from a window of his lodgings, appears 'endlessly growing' and seems a portent of 'London expanding her visionary gates to receive [him], like some dreadful mouth of Acheron' (III, 347).

The inn at Shrewsbury where the young De Quincey observes these ominous portents provides the locale of the third and most interesting scene of transition. He is received here with the same extensive hospitality that he found in Wales, yet a hospitality that has assumed an almost dream-like grandeur and formality:

The wax-lights ... moved pompously before me, as the holy – holy fire, the inextinguishable fire and its golden hearth, moved before Caesar *semper* Augustus, when he made his official or ceremonial *avatars*. Yet still this moved along the ordinary channels of glorification: ... but still the meta- morphosis was not complete. *That* was accomplished when I stepped into the sumptuous room allotted to me. It was a ball-room of noble proportions – lighted, if I chose to issue orders, by three gorgeous chandeliers, not basely wrapped up in paper, but sparkling through all their thickets of crystal branches, and flashing back the soft rays of my tall waxen lights. (III, 345)

The ceremonious procession of lights into the room recalls the ceremo- nious movements of the heavens towards rest in those earlier moments of transition, and perhaps the soft lights shining through 'thickets of crystal branches' suggest the pastoral scene just left behind, though this new pastoral is frozen in a strange formality of artifice. The youth is treated like a Roman emperor, as if his whole journey were meant to lead to some kind of triumphal apotheosis. Viewed in this way, the scene forecasts the enthronement of the 'majestic intellect' which is to come as one of the fruits of the whole journey of experience. But the scene also suggests a ceremonial *rite de passage* to mark a youth's entry into adult experience. De Quincey's progress from the wilderness of Wales to the architectural wilderness of London is presented visually in the chamber's simultaneous suggestion of the solemn natural world left behind and of the solemn city looming ahead. 'The unusual dimensions of the rooms, especially their towering height, brought up continually and obstinately, through natural links of associated feelings or images, the mighty vision of London waiting for me afar off' (III, 346). It is in this room that De Quincey sees and hears the great storm arise that marks the coming of winter and his own passage into the depths of disordered experience.

The roaring voice of warning and nemesis. The moments of delicate equilibrium usually begin with images of fading light and end with auditory images of portentous uproar. This uproar becomes the chief recurrent motif in the narrative for expressing the negative consequences of the youth's rebellion, and it generally represents the threats of a world of disordered experience or the actual destructiveness of that world. The muttered portents of an ominous future are effects which De Quincey both receives from afar and which he half-creates, for the world of hostile experience which threatens to devour him is a world he has willed for himself. The image of the Whispering Gallery in St Paul's Cathedral, to which De Quincey refers frequently in the course of his narrative, is the appropriate embodiment of this situation. The Gallery is an echo chamber which has the power of amplifying 'the softest of whispers' into 'a deafening menace in tempestuous uproars' (III, 296). Elsewhere in the narrative De Quincey explicitly treats the image as a symbolic representation of the 'way the sense and consequences of [his] error [of rebellion] would magnify themselves at every stage of life' (III, 317). Variants of the image of the Whispering Gallery appear in the portentous chamber at Shrewsbury, which in its 'echoing hollowness' amplifies the sounds of the gathering storm (III, 347), and in Brunell's house in London, where the rats make 'a prodigious uproar on the staircase and hall' (III, 355). The motif reappears even in so minor and comic an incident as that which interrupts De Quincey's stealthy escape from the school building, when his trunk ('wilful,' as he is 'wilful' in trying to escape) slips on the staircase and descends 'trundling down from step to step with accelerated pace and multiplying uproar' (III, 299).[6]

The tumultuous uproar reverberates not only from De Quincey's act of assertion, heralding chaotic and uncontrollable consequences, but also from the forces of nemesis which gather to punish that act. The sudden appearance of the Bore on the River Dee, an awesome tidal reversal of the river's normal flow, represents the most salient example of this force of nemesis. Intruding at a point in the narrative when the youth is oppressed by various feelings of guilt, the Bore comes on like a sign of divine vengeance, overturning the normal process of nature with 'a sudden uproar of tumultuous sounds' (III, 305). Although De Quincey and a companion escape drowning, triumph belongs to the river: 'the mighty refluent wash was heard as it rode along, leaving memorials, by sight and by sound, of its victorious power' (III, 307). This dynamic power inevitably recalls the English mail-coach and in a similar way symbolizes all anxieties gathered together into a single externally present form, a mighty power both destructive and punitive. As in the *Mail-Coach*, the roaring force of nemesis finally serves as an embodiment of consciousness divided between a will to power and a sense of victimization. The imagination, which needs to assert its power by freeing itself from external authority, simultaneously realizes the pains of the world of freedom as authority's most potent scourge; imaginative power then allies itself to dread, reconstituting the menace of authority as an internal state of being.[7]

Goals of assertion: figures of deliverance. The narrative progress and the recurrent symbolism outlined above would give to the *Confessions* as a whole a bleak character were it not for the way their gloom sets off and even emphasizes the hero's irrepressible strength of assertion and his ever-renewed faith in attaining a desired form of bliss. De Quincey seeks a projected form of his own imaginative desires, an embodiment of a hypothetical love, offering in response to his assertive power a promise of repose without constriction. Wales, Grasmere, Wordsworth's poetry, opium-eating are all external projections of this imagined form of desire, but its most important embodiments are the comforting women who recur throughout the book. Three of these figures have appeared in the first *Confessions*, the portrait of an unknown lady on the wall of the school-chamber, Ann of Oxford Street, and Margaret, but the type proliferates in the second version, incarnated in such figures as Mrs. Kelsall, a family friend, under whose 'benign superintendence' a 'spirit of love ... diffused itself' throughout the household to which the boy was attached in the days before his hateful schooling (III, 243); Lady Carbery, another family friend, who provides the necessary funds to enable him to flee; the peasant woman on the bank of the River Dee who aids him in a mysterious circumstance, thereby gaining a redemptive suggestiveness as '"the coming woman" born to deliver' him from the 'curse' of pressing anxieties (III, 308); his sister Mary, for whose 'cordiality and ... genial sympathy' he 'stretched out [his] arms' (III, 320, 317). Wife, beloved, sister, stranger, inanimate emblem, these categorical roles in the real world dissolve as if under enchantment and coalesce again in two special roles drawn from the world of romance, the beneficent power from Faery who aids the hero on his quest and the princess at the end of the quest, his reward and comfort.

As one who abets the hero in his journey into the wilderness, the power from Faery may represent, in terms appropriate to a modern romance of inner drama, an externalized projection of that uncanny and life-giving strength of assertion which the hero manages to summon in the face of dismaying circumstance; and the beloved who heals at the end of the journey becomes a projection of the faith that dark experience will yield from its recesses a saving grace of human love. Ann of Oxford Street combines both romance roles; she is a princess under enchantment by the forces of experiential pain, from which the hero seeks to rescue her (and thereby rescue himself); in bestowing healing potions she becomes both a centre for the hero's repose and a source of his renewed vitality; as one who, after this renewal, disappears with a mysterious suddenness from the streets of experience, she suggests the supernatural aide who can give strength to the hero's course but not arrest it, for that course is, imaginatively speaking, without finite bounds.

Goals of assertion: the boundless sea. No one of these figures of grace can grant a permanent repose (even his wife Margaret cannot free De Quincey from the torments of his imagination). It is not simply because figures of comfort tend to slip away from tangible existence into a half-real world of remembered tutelary spirits. The hero is himself responsible for making his repose fitful. He seems compelled to discard previously attained compensations in order to savour experience anew. Wales compensates for the confinements at school, Ann for the trials of London, opium visions for the loss of Ann, but nothing can compensate for the corruption of the visionary imagination by memories of dark experience except further immersion in experience itself. If De Quincey's assertive vitality is to flow into an adequate container, it must flow into that boundless sea and no other. In the *Confessions* the image of the sea is in fact often used to represent protean and unrestricted experience. On the first page of the book the figure of going 'down a shelving beach into a deepening sea' (III, 223) appropriately suggests the imaginative progress of the whole work. The 'mountainous seas' of opium addiction (III, 417), 'the boundless ocean of London' (III, 338), the 'wide, wide world of ocean' (III, 314) on which De Quincey's younger brother Pink literally sets out, in a more drastic imitation of Thomas's flight from authority, are various examples of the unrestricted expanses available to the fugitive from confinement. On a higher level the image of 'the ocean, in everlasting but gentle agitation, ... might not unfitly typify the mind' (III, 395), the ultimate inner expanse that proves to be the locus and the endpoint of all De Quincey's acts of exploration and discovery.

To the passive and frightened man experience is neither so neutral nor so protean. It is a hostile and aggressive force, a devouring sea which invades the land. The Bore thus conveys much the same quality of apocalyptic annihilation, conceived as an influx of experiential chaos, as we find in Wordsworth's dream of the flood in Book V of *The Prelude*.[8] To the free, natural, and assertive man, however, there is no torrent but that of his own individual vitality. In describing the progress of his sleepless nights in London De Quincey provides a paradigm of this idea:

Too generally the very attainment of any deep repose seemed as if mechanically linked to some fatal necessity of self-interruption. It was as though a cup were gradually filled by the sleepy overflow of some natural fountain, the fulness of the cup expressing symbolically the completeness of the rest: but then, in the next stage of the process, it seemed as though the rush and torrent-like babbling of the redundant waters, when running over from every part of the cup, interrupted the slumber which in their earlier stage of silent gathering they had so naturally produced. (III, 355–6)

Few passages are more central to the pattern of life revealed in the book as a whole. The 'natural fountain' may be taken to represent the hero's unrestricted assertive vitality and the cup the haven of repose he seeks in order to alleviate his restlessness. But as soon as he attains complete repose, the haven becomes a confinement, one that is insufficient to contain his vitality. The fountain must overflow into a course directed towards new containers, forever seeking the repose that only a boundless sea can offer. Each convulsive overflow brings De Quincey gasping into wakefulness, but awakening, the emblem of self-revelation, is the master-theme of the book, and the pains of consciousness are the price paid for the development of the majestic intellect and the mature spirit.

2 The progress of the journey

De Quincey's narrative opens with an account of his childhood guardians, a merchant, a magistrate in the industrial suburbs of Manchester, and a plodding, uninspired Low Church clergyman (III, 237–8), all representing the established order of a work-a-day contemporary England, all suggesting an environment hostile to the imagination and the free spirit. At the Manchester Grammar School he enters a more literally constricted environment. The ailments which De Quincey claims arose from his inability to obtain proper exercise are really the physical equivalents of a malaise of the spirit caused by the schoolmaster's inflexible and grinding routine. This schoolmaster, Mr Lawson, appeared in the first *Confessions*, characterized briefly as good-natured but of 'meagre' understanding. Here the portrait is extended and modified, so that the schoolmaster's flaw is not primarily a poverty of intellect but a poverty of imagination and energy. As he plods, tortoise-like, through the day's lessons, Mr Lawson's 'zealotry of conscientiousness,' his 'travelling over the appointed course to the last inch,' his 'rigorous exaction of duties' (III, 273) create an atmosphere as detrimental to imaginative vitality as his excessively long recitation periods are to the students' opportunities for bodily exercise.

After a fourth guardian (inevitably a banker) refuses for various prudent financial reasons to allow his ward to leave the school, De Quincey takes matters into his own hands:

I would elope from Manchester – this was the resolution ... Under that transcendent rapture which the prospect of sudden liberation let loose, all that natural anxiety which should otherwise have interlinked itself with my anticipations was actually drowned in the blaze of joy, as the light of the planet Mercury is lost and confounded on sinking too far within the blaze of the solar beams. Practically I felt no care at all stretching beyond two or three weeks. Not as being heedless and improvident; my tendencies lay generally in the other direction. No; the cause lurked in what Wordsworth, when describing the festal state of France during the happy morning-tide of her First Revolution (1788–1790), calls *'the senselessness of joy'*: this it was, joy – headlong – frantic – irreflective – and (as Wordsworth truly calls it), for that very reason, *sublime* – which swallowed up all capacities of rankling care or heart-corroding doubt. I was, I had been long, a captive: I was in a house of bondage: one fulminating word – *Let there be freedom* – spoken from some hidden recess in my own will, had as by an earthquake rent asunder my prison gates. (III, 278–9)

Joy, De Quincey discovers, is not something that one can beg from a merciful authority. It is won by an act of the will, a triumphant voice, which creates in the very act of articulation an apocalyptic moment destroying the prison-house of the old dispensation. This act of the will represents more than a triumph over the external forces of bondage, for the most constricting bondage is that of the fears within, 'natural anxiety,' 'rankling care,' and 'heart-corroding doubt.' Once he stops dwelling on all the possible dangers suggested by heed, providence, and common sense, he achieves a 'senseless' joy and a 'transcendent rapture.'

The reference to Wordsworth in the passage quoted above is more than casual. De Quincey wants to set out for Grasmere, a pastoral environment 'so much nobler (as Wordsworth notices) in its stern simplicity and continual conflict with danger hidden in the vast draperies of mist overshadowing the hills, and amongst the armies of snow and hail arrayed by fierce northern winters, than the effeminate shepherd's life in the classical Arcadia, or in the flowery pastures of Sicily' (III, 283). De Quincey's new assertive spirit has prompted him to wake with the beauty and terror of nature rather than seek an easy repose. The contrast between Arcadia and the Lake Country, the classical and the romantic, suggests another reason for his choice of destination, for Grasmere means Wordsworth and poetry: 'Inevitably this close connexion of the poetry which most of all had moved me with the particular region and scenery that most of all had fastened upon my affections, and led captive my imagination, was calculated, under ordinary circumstances, to impress upon my fluctuating deliberations a summary and decisive bias' (III, 283). The call of poetry and not the need for exercise, then, is decisive in prompting De Quincey's act. He wants to flee from the rhetoric of the schoolroom to the poetry of experience.

Despite the potency of the Wordsworthian attraction De Quincey does not flee to Grasmere. The regard for Wordsworth's poetry is

too solemn and ... too spiritual, to clothe itself in any hasty or chance movement as at all adequately expressing its strength, or reflecting its hallowed character ... In the present case, under no circumstances should I have dreamed of presenting myself to Wordsworth. The principle of 'veneration' (to speak phrenologically) was by many degrees too strong in me for any such overture on my part. (III, 283–4)

In other words, having chosen Wordsworth as his guide and liberating influence, De Quincey sets him up as a kind of idol who may be approached only through special ceremony. Wordsworth thus becomes an object of fear as well as of desire. It is another instance of De Quincey's tendency to hold back full commitment to a desired experience for fear that it might harden into a new authoritarian imperative. Perhaps it is better to flee in some other direction. Yet this tendency of fear appears even earlier in the passages describing the decision to flee. In the passage of joyous assertion quoted above there is a sinister imagery of drowning, of being 'lost and confounded on sinking too far,' which connects itself with the image of the deepening sea. The decision itself is a piece of 'dark oracular legislation' (III, 278), and the leave-taking is surrounded, as has already been noted, by various symbolic portents of disaster. While De Quincey describes his impulse to flee as a mark of imaginative liberation, he also describes it as an 'inexplicable growth of evil' blighting the 'serene and radiant dawn' of his future prospects (III, 271). He throws off the chains of his prison-house and then carries them along in the form of guilt and fear.

One curious interlude in the narrative, occurring between the boy's flight from school and his return to his mother's home (the end of the first stage of the journey), concentrates these equivocations in so condensed a way that it calls for special attention. On the day before his departure from school the boy receives a letter written in French and addressed to 'Monsieur Monsieur De Quincey':

I was astonished to find myself translated by a touch of the pen not only into a *Monsieur*, but even into a self-multiplied *Monsieur*; or speaking algebraically, into the square of Monsieur; having a chance at some future day of being perhaps cubed into Monsieur. From the letter, as I had hastily torn it open, out dropped a draft upon Smith, Payne, & Smith for somewhere about forty guineas. At this stage of the revelations opening upon me, it might be fancied that the interest of the case thickened: since undoubtedly, if this windfall could be seriously meant for myself, *and no mistake*, never descended upon the head of man, in the outset of a perilous adventure, aid more seasonable, nay, more melodramatically critical. But alas! my eye is quick to value the logic of evil chances. Prophet of evil I ever am to myself: forced for ever into sorrowful auguries that I have no power to hide from my own heart, no, not through one night's solitary dreams. In a moment I saw too plainly I was not Monsieur. (III, 286)

Despite this realization he sets out on his flight with the note in his possession, fearing to return it to the post office lest he thereby reveal his whereabouts to the authorities. The Bore makes its sudden intrusion at this point, presenting a more immediate cause for anxiety, and a solitary peasant woman also appears on the scene to share its danger. After the rushing waters have passed by, De Quincey uses the occasion as an opportunity to entrust the woman with the proper return of his obnoxious monetary burden.

This sequence of incidents, especially when baldly described as here, seems so improbable that it challenges our faith in it as an actual autobiographical occurrence.[9] There is a peculiarly dream-like quality in this succession of strange visitations: tidings of good fortune addressed to the hero, and yet not to the hero but to some stranger who appears to share his identity; an invasion of the sea upon the land; the providential appearance of a kindly Wordsworthian solitary. The dream-like quality, the expansive treatment of so apparently trivial an occasion, the recurrent oscillations in mood between desire and fear – all invite a symbolic reading of the sequence. To recall earlier observations, the Bore and the peasant woman suggest alternatives of nemesis and deliverance, the opposing consequences of the initial act of assertion. If the Bore represents possibilities of disjunction and severance, the encounter with the woman represents the possibility of a renewed human community, so that the two figures on the river bank become 'the Deucalion and Pyrrha of this perilous moment, sole survivors apparently of the deluge' (III, 306). An interpretation of the matter of 'Monsieur Monsieur De Quincey' must remain more conjectural. As a touch of the pen transforms the fugitive boy into 'Monsieur,' and the money offers him the prospect of becoming in the flesh a man of substance ('a chance at some future day of being perhaps cubed into Monsieur'), so is his rebellion a chance for prospective autonomy. The dark side of his imagination, the 'prophet of evil' within him, makes him realize, however, that he is not 'Monsieur' but only a fugitive and his new-found wealth is only a burden of guilt. The whole of this episode embodies the thematic course of the work in miniature, in displaced forms alternatively ludicrous and sublime. Despite the displacement it is easy to observe the typical mutation of opportunities for freedom into sources of anxiety, emblems of anxiety into opportunities for purgation and renewed liberation.

Versions of this sequence repeat themselves during the whole course of the journey to London. De Quincey's initial return to the family homestead is designed to elicit the comforts of his sister Mary, whose support he needs in defending his case for leaving school. Mary is absent, however, and he encounters instead the forbidding figure of his authoritarian mother, who looks on his action with as much equanimity as 'she would have done upon the opening of the seventh seal in the Revelations' (III, 312–13). This ominous apocalyptic image reminds us of the Bore, just as the uproar of that invasion of waters is repeated again in the figure of the Whispering Gallery 'reverberating from the sounding-board within [his] awakened conscience' (III, 313). The ultimate effect of his mother's strictures and his awakened conscience is none the less to prompt his desire to flee again: 'Past all doubt it had now become that the *al fresco* life, to which I had looked with so much hopefulness for a sure and rapid restoration of health, was even more potent than I had supposed it. Literally irresistible it seemed in re-organising the system of my languishing powers' (III, 320). Psychic rather than physical health is once again the real issue here. Though a loving presence might convert a house of bondage into a haven, De Quincey cannot await even the imminent return of the sister he sought, for now only 'wild mountainous and sylvan attractions' (III, 320) can satisfy a reawakened spirit of masculine assertiveness.

De Quincey finds his image of delight in the Welsh countryside: 'Here was the eternal motion of winds and rivers, or of the Wandering Jew liberated from the persecution which compelled him to move and turned his breezy freedom into a killing captivity. Happier life I cannot imagine than this vagrancy, if the weather were but tolerable, through endless successions of changing beauty' (III, 329). This passage soon proves to be ironic, however, in the light of later developments. The pastoral life is beautiful but insufficient to the imagination. De Quincey complains of his 'utter want of access to books, or (generally speaking) to any intellectual intercourse. I languished all the day through, and all the week through – with nothing whatever … to relieve my mortal ennui' (III, 339). He becomes captive to his own assertive impulse, and the ideal of the Wandering Jew released from persecution becomes reversed as the region of 'breezy freedom' turns indeed into a 'killing captivity.' The voice in De Quincey that desires repose thus speaks of

some overmastering fiend, some instinct of migration, sorrowful but irresistible, ... driving me forth to wander like the unhappy Io of the Grecian
mythus, some oestrus of hidden persecution that bade me fly when no man
pursued – not in false hope, for my hopes whispered but a doubtful chance –
not in reasonable fear, for all was sweet pastoral quiet and autumnal beauty
around me, – suddenly I took a fierce resolution to sacrifice my weekly
allowance, to slip my anchor, and to throw myself in desperation upon
London.   (III, 338)

The 'fierce resolution,' evaluated so negatively here, is part of a continuing thrust of energy and desire for new experience, which has been present since the beginning of the narrative. Each successive environment
eventually seems inadequate to contain the natural fountain of the
youth's restless will. The series of tentative goals adopted at successive
stages of the journey – an opportunity for mid-day recreation, a placid
home-life in the company of his sister, the beauties of the Welsh landscape, and, finally, the intellectual and social attractions of the metropolis – indicate the increasing range of the youth's interests and the
increasing autonomy of his strength. Yet despite this pattern of linear
and incremental development an inescapable circularity of progress
manifests itself throughout. It becomes increasingly difficult to distin-
guish the forms of liberation from those of captivity, because two opposing
voices, one attached to order and one to assertive autonomy, comment
alternately on each experience. Each stage of the journey is viewed pro-
spectively as a haven from the previous stage, then as a new constriction,
and, retrospectively, as a spot of innocence now lost. The final stage
completes the circle, for in London the journeying youth finds another
city of pain, another Manchester like the one from which he originally
fled.

3 Renewal of the 1822 'Confessions'

The narration of these London experiences represents another kind of
return as well, for now De Quincey arrives at that portion of his story
told long before in the first version of the Confessions of 1822, and the
rest of the book substantially follows this early version. In encountering
this material for a second time one receives the remarkable impression of
a seamless thematic and narrative continuity between the book's new
and vastly extended prologue and its old, unchanged centre and climax.
It is as if all the seeds of De Quincey's late understanding of his experi-

ences were there from the start, awaiting their opportunity to germinate, so effortlessly do the story of Ann and the alternative narcotic visions carry out the thematic implications of the vicissitudes of the journey. Yet the new material alters the significance of the old even as it assimilates it, or rather a significance always present but not salient becomes so now.

One reason for this ease of assimilation of the old and the new is that the symbols and episodes of the version of 1822, though vivid, are indeterminate in significance, for they have few contextual roots, few overt links with the author's evaluations of his own experience. The more detailed context of events and attitudes presented in the second version both enriches and particularizes the meanings of emblems too loosely suggestive in their first appearance. Moreover the general structure of mood and theme in the version of 1822 invites the kind of refining specificity that the second version renders. To recall some points made in chapter 2, De Quincey in 1822 gives little sense of himself as an individual, so that his history has simple archetypal proportions, the passage of an individual from an innocence associated with a sense of community to an experiential solitude where one's only companion is an imagination that mirrors alternate moods of aggrandizement and desolation. The problematic relation between community and solitude remains of course as a dominant theme in the *Confessions* of 1856, but its generalized features are now brought to bear upon the specific situation of the author's own individuality.

One point clarified in the second version is that there is no temporally prior state of innocence existing either in one's environment or in oneself. The new narrative presents us virtually at its outset with a youth perpetually impelled towards separation from any kind of established community in which he finds himself, either to set forth on his own in isolated freedom or to find reciprocal loves. The dismal portents of desolation – the Whispering Gallery, the Bore, the storm in Shrewsbury – penetrate the narration of the early experience and establish the presence of external threat and personal anxiety long before the hero reaches London. There is little that the narration of the London episodes and the opium-eating can do but continue the cycles of mood and behaviour already established in the extended prefatory narration added in 1856, though it heightens their intensity and distils their energizing principles in massed, opposing visions.

The mood of the 1856 *Confessions* is closest to that of the version of 1822 in those moments which emphasize a quest for repose and responsive love; hence the episode involving Ann of Oxford Street needs no commentary beyond that offered in chapter 2. Such additions as De Quincey does make in 1856 to the London narrative all tend to further a contrasting emphasis on experiential vicissitudes and their consequences. There is, for example, a much fuller portrait of the disreputable lawyer Brunell, in whose 'hunger-bitten' house (III, 351) the youth lodges. As master of a house of deprivation and an adept in the labyrinthine world of the legal system Brunell should stand schematically in the same position as Mr Lawson, the guardians, and De Quincey's mother as a figure of obstruction and bondage. Yet in the portrayal of the lawyer there are no hints of tyranny and persecuting enmity. Far from representing a narrow order, he has gone deep into the protean world of experience himself, which has had a humanizing effect on him, as De Quincey shows in an appraisal both acute and filled with pathos:

From the expression of his face, but much more from the contradictory and self-counteracting play of his features, you gathered in a moment that he was a man who had much to conceal, and much, perhaps, that he would gladly forget. His eye expressed wariness against surprise, and passed in a moment into irrepressible glances of suspicion and alarm. No smile that ever his face naturally assumed but was pulled short up by some freezing counteraction, or was chased by some close-following expression of sadness. One feature there was of relenting goodness and nobleness in Mr. Brunell's character ... He had the deepest, the most liberal, and unaffected love of knowledge, but, above all, of that specific knowledge which we call literature. (III, 350–1)

The expressions which cross Brunell's face, brittle strength constantly besieged by harrowing fears, warmth quelled by the tyrannies of his knowledge or sobered by the memory of loss, remind us tellingly of emotions everywhere present in the author himself. Brunell's literary interests, the pursuit of which was interrupted by circumstances forcing him into his present 'stormy (and no doubt oftentimes disgraceful) career in life' (III, 351), provide another link with De Quincey's own highest aspirations. It is as if in meeting Brunell, another man who failed, as it were, to take the road to Grasmere or its equivalent, the young hero has come face to face with a hypothetical and proleptic self-portrait, and there is much in De Quincey's own career of incessant furtive movement and elusive postures to suggest the portrait's veracity. Brunell and Ann come to represent in the second *Confessions* projected forms of the poles of De Quincey's imaginative self-awareness, one representing an undiminished faith in the possible resurrections of innocence, the other a restless consciousness of unending experiential dangers. The scenes with Ann still represent the epiphanic centre of the *Confessions*, but the augmented role of Brunell in the second version provides a sobering and necessary counterbalance, one consonant with the more ironic mood of self-evaluation present in De Quincey's late autobiographical writings.

The contrary principles represented by Brunell and Ann repeat themselves in other figurations in the latter part of the book. They are present in the relation between the suffering little girl living in Brunell's house and the youth himself, the one able to sleep despite her suffering, the other forever fitfully waking (III, 355–6). In describing this incident, first presented in 1822, De Quincey now adds that account of his own restlessness, expressed in the figure of a cup filled with 'redundant waters,' which we have glanced at earlier in this chapter. This addition serves, as does the augmented description of Brunell, to emphasize the theme of experiential knowledge, ceaselessly wearying and ceaselessly pursued. Such additions also clarify the meaning of later passages in the work, carried over from the version of 1822. One such passage describes a strange confrontation at the door of De Quincey's cottage in Grasmere between his own lovely servant girl and a wandering Malay:

Her native spirit of mountain intrepidity contended with the feeling of simple awe which her countenance expressed as she gazed at the tiger-cat before her. A more striking picture there could not be imagined than the beautiful English face of the girl, and its exquisite bloom, together with her erect and independent attitude, contrasted with the sallow and bilious skin of the Malay, veneered with mahogany tints by climate and marine air, his small, fierce, restless eyes, thin lips, slavish gestures and adorations.   (III, 403–4)

In the first version this confrontation seems thematically gratuitous though powerful in its hold upon De Quincey's imagination, as if it needed only the enlarged context of the *Confessions* of 1856 to release its latent meanings. Observing the tense scene depicted in this passage, De Quincey is in the position of a dreamer who stands apart from an action and yet identifies with one (or both) of its participants. The servant girl seems to be another Ann, but purified in her exemption from experiential pain. Innocent but with an 'independent attitude' and a 'native spirit of mountain intrepidity,' she concentrates in herself those values of beauty, assertive strength, and freedom which De Quincey desired to find in the Lake Country when he ran away from school and actually found for a time in his wanderings through Wales. The Malay is more problematic, for if his appearance is one more manifestation of the loathsome Other in De Quincey's writings, another crocodile among the roses, his 'restless eyes' and his exotic gesturing remind us strangely of Brunell; as he soon proves to be both an opium-eater and in need of 'respite from the pains of wandering' (III, 405), he reminds us of the hero himself. The confrontation between the Malay and the servant girl thus becomes an emblem of the polarities within De Quincey's own record of physical experience, exuberant health and weariness, and of the polarities within his imagination, an innocence ever strong and a fear of the dark unknown that becomes what it beholds.

This scene, then, is another version of those confrontations at the threshold which recur throughout De Quincey's writings, Macbeth and Macduff, Williams and the servant girl from the 'Postscript' to *Murder*, the coach and the gig. Viewed in the context of its final setting in the extended *Confessions*, it acquires a significance that clarifies the meaning of all the rest. For this confrontation with the dark Other is ultimately a confrontation with the imagined face of one's own strange consciousness, so terrifying in its autonomy, its evasion of order, that it becomes distorted into a loathsome mask. De Quincey's dread of external powers, embodied in works like the *Mail-Coach* and 'System of the Heavens,' is a variant of this terror, although invocations of the deity in those works link horror with an overriding order. Any connection of the self with power, whether it comes from without in ordered or disordered forms or whether it manifests itself as an energy from within, is frightening. Thus Brunell, the Malay, and later the imagined figure of the labouring Piranesi, perpetually climbing towards self-renewing confrontations with the abyss, are all fearsome types of the wandering protagonist, feverishly and elaborately coping with the intricacies of an externality restlessly sought.

The successive types of this figure become increasingly sinister and yet increasingly close to De Quincey's own dream images, as if he were rounding upon a confrontation with the dark power of his will by an indirect route. The shifty figure of Brunell mediates between the wandering English opium-eater and the Malayan opium-eater, and the latter becomes the link to the Oriental nightmares of 'The Pains of Opium': 'The Malay has been a fearful enemy for months. Every night, through his means, I have been transported into Asiatic scenery' (III, 441). We should re-examine this scenery, observed once before in the first version of the *Confessions*, in the light of the thematic emphases of the second:

I was stared at, hooted at, grinned at, chattered at, by monkeys, by paroquets, by cockatoos. I ran into pagodas, and was fixed for centuries at the summit, or in secret rooms; I was the idol; I was the priest; I was worshipped; I was sacrificed. I fled from the wrath of Brama through all the forests of Asia; Vishnu hated me; Seeva lay in wait for me. I came suddenly upon Isis and Osiris: I had done a deed, they said, which the ibis and the crocodile trembled at. Thousands of years I lived and was buried in stone coffins, with mummies and sphinxes, in narrow chambers at the heart of eternal pyramids. I was kissed, with cancerous kisses, by crocodiles, and was laid, confounded with all unutterable abortions, amongst reeds and Nilotic mud. (III, 442-3)

In the first version it seemed as if these dream images were the issue of a desperate attempt by the imagination to establish some kind of connection with the forces of power, however horrid, in the face of an even more horrid fear of isolation and personal inconsequence. But the extended preliminary narration of the second version enables us to see in addition that such dreams are simply exotic transformations of elements in De Quincey's own past experience, the confining crypt-like rooms in Manchester, the panicked flight, the uprising of nature against him in the form of the Bore, the ever-present figures of authoritarian disapproval. Ultimately, however, the references point inward as well as to external experience, for in a sense all of these demonic figures are versions of himself. He becomes a mummy along with other mummies, and when he dwells with the crocodiles they treat him as a brother. He too is a Hindu god as well as a votary of his own image, and if the figure of the Malay has spawned all these images, the peculiar mix of loathing for and self-identification with that figure reaches its intense fruition here. The presiding god of his nightmares proves to be inseparable from his own identity, self-consuming and shivering into a multitude of subsidiary identifications, just as the presiding impulse of his own assertive will has generated all of the various dark consequences of his own experience.

In tracing a particular thematic strand I have temporarily by-passed 'The Pleasures of Opium,' but the detour serves to reinforce the essential point to be gathered from all the opium visions in the revised *Confessions*: that the extended introductory narrative of the youth's experiences illuminates the visionary material, showing it to be a mirror of the self in the sum of its experiences and desires. In the great reverie-transformed scene above Liverpool harbour there are a few additions and revisions in 1856 which stress this equation and emphasize the multiplicities of experience: 'all through the hours of night, I have continued motionless, as if frozen, without consciousness of myself as an object anywise distinct from the multiform scene which I contemplated from above. Such a scene in all its elements was not unfrequently realised for me on the gentle eminence of Everton. Obliquely to the left lay the many-languaged town of Liverpool; obliquely to the right, the multitudinous sea' (III, 395). These new sentences realize the full potentialities of the first version of the description. Not only does the scene remain 'somewhat typical of what took place in [the] reverie,' but there is a virtual assertion of identity between subjective and objective experience; in one sense the scene is entirely mind and in another the mind is wholly absorbed in externality.[10] The varied nature of this externality, moreover, here receives particular stress in such terms as 'multiform scene,' the 'scene in all its elements,' 'many-languaged town,' 'multitudinous sea.' No matter what image plays before the expanded vision of the opium-eater, whether demonic or paradisal, he cannot escape apprehension of a mirrored self, drawing its completed form from an inextricable reciprocity between multiple external encounters and a subjective principle of unceasing activity.

This point becomes clarified in the second version of the *Confessions*, which provides the context for an assimilation of De Quincey's original reflections on Liverpool harbour into the work's thematic and narrative content. The many-languaged city and the mulitudinous sea appear in this context as symbols of the journey itself in its experiential and psychic dimensions: 'The town of Liverpool represented the earth, with its sorrow and its graves left behind, yet not out of sight, nor wholly forgotten. The ocean, in everlasting but gentle agitation, yet brooded over by dove-like calm, might not unfitly typify the mind, and the mood which then swayed it' (III, 395). The main narrative sequence in this book describes wandering that began in one city and ended in another, and each city marks the site of 'sorrows' and 'graves' left behind temporally but in another sense not left behind at all. In Manchester the youth experienced the first sorrow of consciousness, the rising of an assertive self against outward restriction, and 'closed the door for ever' (III, 297) on a portrait emblematic of quasi-divine protection and love in order to begin his terrestrial wandering. In London this wandering brought him to Ann and, more important, to the experience of her loss. Subsequent wandering, occurring chiefly in the worlds of narcotic vision, brings him to the city of this vision, which is as much an emblem of the past recaptured in a mood of total acceptance as it is an emblem of some desired repose. The image of the sea functions here as symbol of the psychic matrix in which all experiential goals and experiential losses are located. This sea is boundless, resistant to definition in terms of direction or goal. Its principle of being resides in its own 'everlasting but gentle agitation,' its protean indeterminacy. Gentleness and a 'dove-like calm,' as of the Miltonic Holy Spirit, are not necessary concomitants to agitation of mind (as 'The Pains of Opium' show). What joins them here is a special and saving unification of activity and understanding. The two consummating terms in which the whole passage ends, 'infinite activities, infinite repose,' must be understood as existing in a dialectical relation. To know that one's psychic activity is 'infinite,' that there is no point of rest, no sweet golden clime of permanent attainment, to know this totally and clearly, is the only repose there is, the only inviolable repose. Knowledge of the whole creates a distance from the sometimes painful consequences of the parts, effecting a 'resting from human labours' that permits an unimpeded flow of quasi-divine energy.

These attained harmonies cast 'The Pains of Opium' that follow in a problematic light. There one encounters agitation without repose, and one may wonder whether De Quincey has somehow let a privileged moment of understanding slip away. It is better, however, to regard the visions of pain not as a diminishment of insight but as a completion of insight. What one apprehends in moments of sublime intuition about the self and its experience may offer an infinite repose to the spirit, but in the context of daily life this apprehension is often painful. Hence the same quality of indeterminacy, endless movement, and, by implication, endless loss of any finite bliss, found in the vision of Liverpool harbour, is repeated in darker hues in the visions of Piranesi labouring, of heavenly cities transforming themselves into urban swarms weltering in the sea (a dissolution of the delicate balance of city and sea achieved in the vision at Everton), of defeat in some final, apocalyptic battle resulting in 'everlasting farewells' for all that one has loved. The exquisite tranquillity that pervades the scene at Liverpool represents De Quincey's sense of the supreme worth of his knowledge, but the later visions represent its cost.

The pathos of such a double vision is that there is no way of bridging the gulf between the sensed worth of total knowledge and its sensed cost. The former is available only in moments out of time, moments of complete and receptive awareness, whereas the latter is generated only by experience in time, a cumulative record of all those objects of desire attained and then lost, each in its turn. The visions of loss in 'The Pains of Opium' render this irony, that the moments of sublime awareness themselves are indeed only moments, points of finite bliss (though infinite to the consciousness for the duration of the moment) in the long continuum of experience that stretches before and after. What these dark visions have in common in their presentations of crumbling cities, dissolving pastorals, and lost battles is a rendering of the decay of the apocalyptic ideal, the faith that imagination itself can create out of the pains of experience a resolution to all contraries, a dazzling integrative construct like the dream-cathedral in *The English Mail-Coach*. Imagination, in the form of the clarifying visions of 'The Pains of Opium,' is at last employed in a critique of itself, in a fierce questioning whether its comforts can make any greater claim to permanency than the comforts offered by Ann of Oxford Street or Indian summer in Wales. This entirely reverses the tendency of the *Suspiria* and the *Mail-Coach* to depict imagination as an unequivocal salvation, which the figure of a destroying and creating God is introduced to ratify. De Quincey was perhaps too close to the actuality of his experience when he wrote these passages in the first *Confessions* to allow himself recourse to such figures of absolute comfort, and at the end of his creative life he does not, in revising the *Confessions*, betray his earlier honesty. At this point he knows what he has always sensed (for even the musical structure that supports the 'Dream-Fugue' hints at artifice), that there is no apocalypse for the natural self, only continuity.

And I awoke in struggles, and cried aloud, 'I will sleep no more! (III, 447)

This cry, which concludes the final dream-vision in the *Confessions*, has greater resonance than when we first considered it, a resonance gathered not only from the expanded implications of the second *Confessions* but also from the major works written between the first and second versions. De Quincey has perpetually sought through the course of his writings, on the one hand, an attainment of unrestricted power and, on the other, a return to the harmonious repose of early innocence. In such works as the *Suspiria* and the *Mail-Coach* the second sleep of the opium-dream compensates for the lost early repose and offers as well a revelation of a giant, all-comprehending consciousness, so as to merge both goals. But the movement of the *Confessions*, to repeat a suggestion made earlier in this commentary, tends perpetually in the direction of awakening, awakening from any situation of stasis, whether baleful or benign, and in this awakening the writer's integrity as a human being is preserved. Too intense a consciousness of contraries, as manifested in both 'The Pleasures of Opium' and 'The Pains of Opium,' proves to be yet another form of bondage, a final threat to that integrity. Thus in triumphing, as he says he does, over opium addiction (III, 447) De Quincey triumphs over imagination itself and re-enters the world of ordinary experience.

It is perhaps strange to speak of the departure of a Romantic writer from the hold of his imagination as a triumph, but in the concluding pages of De Quincey's imaginative history there is little sense of the typical Romantic palinode written in dejection. There is strength not only in what remains behind (De Quincey speaks of the residual 'firmness' which he was still able to muster in conquering his addiction [III, 447], a new version of the old assertive strength) but also in what lies ahead, the possibility of his mature renewal in the paths of experience. Thus the convulsive waking from his imagination does not represent a spiritual death but rather a rebirth:

Lord Bacon conjectures that it may be painful to be born as to die. That seems probable; and, during the whole period of diminishing the opium, I had the torments of a man passing out of one mode of existence into another, and liable to the mixed or the alternate pains of birth and death. The issue was not death, but a sort of physical regeneration; and I may add that ever since, at intervals, I have had a restoration of more than youthful spirits. (III, 448)

The convention maintained in the *Confessions* of discussing mental states in terms of physical allows 'physical regeneration' to imply psychic regeneration as well. His spirits are restored in 'more than youthful' form, by which, of course, De Quincey means something other than the spirits of childhood. The springs of youth, with their suggestion of an innocent assertiveness, return to flow with a calm which transcends youthful buoyancy, the calm of an experienced sanity, not so sublime as some of those past moments of self-transcendence brought on by the integrating imagination, but more durable and ultimately more satisfactory.

In one respect the ending of the *Confessions* of 1856 deviates from this affirmation of the openness of experience. Having achieved his own regeneration, De Quincey apparently cannot bear the thought of leaving Ann behind in the horrors of experience, though for her the only route of egress is through the gate of death. In the appended story, 'The Daughter of Lebanon,' a piece left-over from the *Suspiria*, Ann reappears in the guise of a spiritually innocent and wronged prostitute of Damascus whom St Luke promises to restore to her father's house. The promise is fulfilled with deadly exactitude, for a plague strikes the city, the stricken Daughter acknowledges her spiritual obligations, the heavens open, and she is indeed received into her 'Father's House' (III, 456). The piece unpleasantly recalls the worst vein of Victorian piety, but more important it strikes a dissonant note in relation to the rest of the conclusion of the *Confessions*. As the embodiment of a protective love Ann's final place is more appropriately in the devouring world of experience that separates her forever from De Quincey's life. She is an emblem of loss, and it is no part of the imaginative scheme of the conclusion to exclude a sense of lost bliss or a recollection of dreadful experience from the protagonist's mature calm. Hence De Quincey's original ending is much more satisfactory than the later appendage, much more the inevitable ending. He retains in dreams images of his lost innocence and his dreadful ordeal, informed by one final Miltonic reference: Adam and Eve's last retrospective glance at Paradise, ' "With dreadful faces thronged and fiery arms" ' (III, 449). For De Quincey this scene perhaps represents a palimpsest of his oppressive imagination of contraries. At every stage of the journey recorded in the second *Confessions* there was a Paradise to be left behind – the moments with Ann, the last day in Wales, even the vesper service at school on the evening of the youth's departure. Paradise so readily lost is perhaps best lost once and for all, and this can come only with the abandonment of that ultimate intoxication, the visionary imagination in which De Quincey invested virtually all his faith as a measure of his value as an artist and as a man. There is compensation for this melancholy insight in the notion implicit in it of an open-ended freedom of experiential possibilities. Though in every way as eloquent as the bravura pieces of the 1840s, as fully attuned to the dialectic of contraries and the possibilities of visionary transcendence, the second *Confessions* is closer finally to the demythologizing *Autobiographic Sketches*. Looking back further, one finds the most genuine affinities with those unlikely narratives about Tartars and Spanish Nuns, who foreshadow the hero of this final self-quest as wanderers ultimately at home in their homelessness.

❧[7]❧

Epilogue: De Quincey's Place in the Romantic Tradition

De Quincey begins and ends his literary work in awe of the imagination's power but sceptical of its sufficiency. There are at various points in his career attempts to find perspectives where imaginative power becomes wholly sufficient to personal desires, as in the visionary autobiography of the *Suspiria* or the multi-levelled synthesis of the *Mail-Coach*, but in the end mere existence in experience appears to survive the visionary quest as if that were just another of the opium-dreams from which one wakes. Frank Kermode has called De Quincey's visions 'fake ends' and goes on to credit him with understanding 'the horror ... of modern form, the place where we accept the knowledge that our inherited ways of echoing the structure of the world have no concord with it, but only, and then under conditions of great difficulty, with the desires of our own minds.'[1] This observation closely fits the *Confessions* (though 'horror' scarcely describes the fullness of De Quincey's complex awareness), for the work summons up extravagant visionary forms which prove to be tautologous mirrors of a perplexity that survives the dissolution of the forms themselves. Even the other major visionary works hint at an incongruity between lived experience and imaginative shapings. The *Suspiria*, as we recall, founders upon this very incongruity, discovering that it cannot do justice to both self and pattern in a single coherent work, and *The English Mail-Coach* succeeds aesthetically by postulating a kind of gnostic universe where everything equates to its opposite, where every horror is a glory, every abyss a mighty house of the Lord, every experiential chaos a secret index of apocalyptic unification. All the opposites cancel each other and leave a void. Ambiguity confronts us, then, wherever we turn in De Quincey's work, whether in those places of centripetal visionary synthesis or those which subject such synthesis to a sceptical critique. Neither situation provides a suitable basis for the affirmation of any particular moral imperative or any particular world-view, positive or negative. De Quincey the man and journalist of course has distinctive opinions (and crotchets), but as an imaginative writer he seems possessed by the need to evade statement, as if he were essentially incapable of faith.

Thus the unknown power that haunts De Quincey's prose of vision tends to slip in and out of successive masks – sometimes appearing as God, sometimes as the forces of the world, sometimes as the artist's imagination; perhaps all these guises are manifestations of one underlying reality, or perhaps there is no such reality and the masks are fictions, vehicles without a tenor. Born of Romantic idealism and Romantic scepticism, intensely nurtured in De Quincey's own anxieties and needs, these equivocations have subsequently enjoyed a significant literary life. When we note his passing visions of an inscrutable and ironic deity, of labyrinthine passages through experience, and of arcane correspondences in which 'the least things in the universe must be secret mirrors to the greatest' (I, 129), we are reminded, not accidentally, of Borges, who is fond of De Quincey and quotes the line about 'secret mirrors' in an essay on the Cabbalistic tradition.[2] As we take a selective glance backward at the literary ancestry of the great Argentine master of this tradition, through Mallarmé and Baudelaire on the transcendental side and Chesterton, Stevenson, and Wilkie Collins on the ratiocinative or 'labyrinthine' side, we find De Quincey, along with Poe (who learned much from the *Confessions*), as a strong progenitor. The progress of literary generations of course exercises a refining influence, producing in Borges a writer whose prose is as cool, finely wrought, and pointed as De Quincey's is 'impassioned,' meandering, and prolix. But the differences cannot obscure an essential continuity of effect, one in which the High Romantic endeavour to discover transcendence in experience is fondly entertained so as to be sceptically judged. There is more apparent faith in De Quincey, more irony in Borges, yet even a work as early as the first version of the *Confessions* may be viewed as a prophetic synopsis of this progress from faith to irony, moving as it does from a sense of communal innocence in the 'Preliminary Confessions,' rising to the High Romantic faith in a 'majestic intellect' or expansive imagination, only to descend into a labyrinthine nightmare world of mockery from which one desperately needs to escape.

The world we experience becomes labyrinthine only if we credit it with the defining characteristic of all labyrinths, a secret design behind its local complexities. When the writer projects designs of order, bred in the imagination, on the complexities of experience, he creates secondary labyrinths in his art, discovering in apparent blind alleys passages of the true way. These creations perform for the writer a double service: in so far as they mimic and expose the design of that larger labyrinth, the world, they testify to the grandeur of the writer as a seer; but if the design of the world should happen to remain undisclosed after all, then his creations serve as a place of refuge from the outer mystery, for they at least possess a design *he knows*. From the vortexes of Urizen in Blake, to the gardens of Xanadu in Coleridge and the Arab's shell in Wordsworth, to the dream-cathedrals of De Quincey and the Great Wheels of Yeats, literature in the Romantic tradition is filled with microcosmic structures pretending to comprehend the outer cosmos while labouring to keep it at bay. There is much in these creations that is valuable – beauties of expression and form that give pleasure to our sensibilities, complexities of concept that exercise and exhilarate the mind – but much that is deserving of scepticism, as their authors themselves frequently give us to understand. For the world may not be labyrinthine after all, only various, and by projecting a sense of design on the world the imagination creates the very craving for solutions that it offers to satisfy. This syndrome manifests itself with peculiar force in De Quincey's writings, and in these writings there is a fine line between that which simply reproduces the syndrome, and that which diagnoses it, between imaginative structures displayed as havens of the soul and structures displayed as 'fakes.'

But there is another, redeeming side to imaginative activity, not to be found in the virtuosity of its structures, but in its attestation to personal vitality and self-renewing hope in the face of perplexity. This study has referred to Wordsworth far more often than to Poe, Baudelaire, or Borges, and not from any critical predilection on my part for stressing sources rather than influences. In the poems of Wordsworth that we continue to admire, imagination is a force that impels the poet into wayfaring, into exploring the indeterminacies of the self and of outward experience; it provides 'Blank misgivings of a Creature / Moving about in worlds not realised,' the hope of 'something evermore about to be,' the poignant faith that enables him to quiz his own transcendental meditations and yet to trust the value of his experiential encounters: 'If this be but a vain belief, yet oh! ... How often has my spirit turned to thee.'[3] These lines could provide fit epigraphs for the *Confessions*, for the whole enterprise of De Quincey's ever renewed self-scrutinies, and for what is moving in his strenuous attempts, in the face of probable failure, to fashion to the shapes of outward darkness into images adequate to desire. One notes as well De Quincey's affinities with Romantic figures temperamentally more remote like Shelley and Keats, who, in confronting their own apocalyptic chariots of annihilation or dream-temples commemorating wars in heaven, remain sufficiently self-aware to ask what their own roles in these visions may be and what value there is to their knowledge. Imagined universes of mysterious and equivocal powers become mainly a backdrop for manifestations of personal explorative energies.

Although De Quincey lacks the massive self-trust of writers greater than himself, such as Wordsworth, this energy is manifest in his restlessness, his refusal to surrender to his burdens. The astonishing point to be made about his writings, in view of his reputation for neuraesthenic incapacity (partly a self-created persona) and the real debilitating force of his addiction, is the enterprise that they reveal. Working in a literary medium largely unsuited to his introspective and visionary temperament, he makes and remakes versions of himself and his spiritual history, versions of his visions; he is always failing and always returning for new attempts. There is something at once exasperating and heroic in his literary technique, in his displays of rhetorical agility and his strategies of displacement designed so that he may entice and elude us, a technique only less remarkable than the naked voice of self-revelation which tends suddenly to break through these displays. If De Quincey is not a writer of the first rank, he refuses to be merely trivial, a minor success, to be no more than a technician of prose style, a raconteur, a tour-guide into the exotic. Behind these external forms we sense the constant presence of a figure balanced on a pivot between visionary transcendence and the absurd void, knowing that that precarious point is his true place, for all his searching, and the exemplification of his humanity. He is one of the last writers upon whom the tradition of the apocalyptic vision maintains its hold more or less in traditional form, one of the first in whom the spiritual journey of the self assumes its familiar modern guise. The historical importance of his imaginative writings resides in their embodying one of the literary moments in which these venerable traditions become transformed from expressions of the way to truth into reflexive emblems of consciousness. Their poignancy resides in the shadowy but still noble recollecton they offer of the imaginative wellsprings from which they derive.

⚗ Notes ⚗

NOTES TO CHAPTER 1

1 De Quincey's imagery has attracted the attention of almost all critics who have treated his work from a literary standpoint. For discussions and catalogues of De Quincey's most frequently recurring images and motifs see Lane Cooper, *The Prose Poetry of Thomas De Quincey* (Leipzig: Verlag von Dr. Seele 1902), p 18; Françoise Moreux, *Thomas De Quincey: la vie, l'homme, l'œuvre* (Paris: Presses universitaires de France 1964), pp 554–8; Elisabeth Schneider, *Coleridge, Opium, and Kubla Khan* (Chicago: University of Chicago Press 1953), pp 77–80; Alethea Hayter, *Opium and the Romantic Imagination* (Berkeley: University of California Press 1968), pp 235–54; and especially J. Hillis Miller, *The Disappearance of God: Five Nineteenth-Century Writers* (Cambridge, Mass: Harvard University Press 1963), pp 17–80.
2 The most extensive and valuable treatment of De Quincey from this perspective appears in Miller, *The Disappearance of God*. See especially pp 24–5 for a discussion of the imagery of desolation.
3 *Blackwood's Edinburgh Magazine*, 57 (June 1845), 749–50.
4 The best comments on the nature of De Quincey's autobiographical writings are made by Roger J. Porter, who remarks that the autobiographer presents 'a character in search of himself, journeying toward understanding even while he recognizes that this may be an impossible quest to fulfill,' and he notes in De Quincey specifically 'the confrontation of an ideal self, one wished for and planned, with another self that cannot meet these expectations' ('The Double Self: Autobiography and Literary Form in Gibbon, De Quincey, Gosse and Edwin Muir' [unpublished diss. Yale 1967], pp 20, 21).
5 This creative enterprise corresponds essentially to the critical endeavour of such students of non-fictional prose as George Levine and William

Madden to find appropriate terms for discussing the imaginative element in that genre: 'The terms of the tentative poetics of non-fiction ... disclose a hierarchy of kinds of prose, a scale of aesthetic perfection, on which, as we ascend, the distinctions between meaning and language tend to disappear ... As we approach the top of the scale, we find a prose ... increasingly marked by a distinctive voice, increasingly self-contained and inward-looking, increasingly shifting its referent from an assumed outward reality to an open consciousness seeking to organize its understanding of a complex experience in language' ('Introduction,' *The Art of Victorian Prose*, ed. Levine and Madden [New York: Oxford University Press 1968], pp xvii–xviii).

6 Recent critics of De Quincey have tended to regard these peculiar characteristics of his prose as an attempt to avoid confrontation with deeply imagined threats and sensed desolations. See Miller, *The Disappearance of God*, pp 38–41; and Robert M. Adams, who notes De Quincey's odd kind of resourcefulness: 'Though he has only the phantasm of a plan, and proceeds only indirectly by sidewise methods of digression and analogy, yet the effect of his strange beetle-like activity is somehow to fill up a previously hollow void of experience' (*Nil: Episodes in the Literary Conquest of the Void During the Nineteenth Century* [New York: Oxford University Press 1966], p 37).

7 These imaginative possibilities lie not only in subject-matter original to De Quincey but also in source material – often prosaic – borrowed from others, as Albert Goldman has impressively shown in *The Mine and the Mint: Sources for the Writings of Thomas De Quincey* (Carbondale: Southern Illinois University Press 1965). According to Goldman: 'The workings of De Quincey's imagination ... always have a certain consistency, whether acting on the stuff of his experience, dreams, and fantasies or whether assimilating and transforming such literary materials as memoirs, books, newspaper reports, and personal documents' (pp 82–3).

8 *The Prelude or the Growth of a Poet's Mind*, ed Ernest de Selincourt, 2nd ed, rev Helen Darbishire (Oxford: Clarendon Press 1959), XIV, 101–2 (1850). Subsequent references to *The Prelude* are incorporated in the text in parentheses.

9 The rapprochement of prose and verse fostered by Wordsworth on the one side and writers like De Quincey and Lamb on the other is discussed by Travis R. Merritt, 'Taste, Opinion, and Theory in the Prose of Victorian Stylism,' Levine and Madden, eds, *The Art of Victorian Prose*, pp 4 ff. For a more detailed account of Lamb's version of this rapprochement see Fred V. Randel, *The World of Elia: Charles Lamb's Essayistic Romanticism*

(Port Washington, NY: Kennikat Press 1975), pp 3 ff, an exemplary treatment of Romantic non-fictional prose as imaginative art.

NOTES TO CHAPTER 2

1 See, e.g., 'Night,' lines 25–34. That De Quincey was at least aware of Blake we know from an off-hand reference to him as a 'fine mystic' (*Collected Writings*, II, 400) in an essay dated 1840. Whether he knew of Blake when he was writing the *Confessions* cannot be determined.
2 This kind of reading has been offered most recently by Hayter, *Opium and the Romantic Imagination*, where De Quincey's dream images are considered as symbolic representations of opium addiction itself. See p 249 f.
3 'The Garden,' lines 43–4 (*The Poems and Letters of Andrew Marvell*, ed H.M. Margoliouth [Oxford: Clarendon Press 1952], vol I).
4 For a study of De Quincey's knowledge of the unpublished MSS of *The Prelude* see John E. Wells, 'De Quincey and *The Prelude* in 1839,' *Philological Quarterly*, 20 (January 1941), 1–24. My essay '"The Type of a Mighty Mind": Mutual Influence in Wordsworth and De Quincey,' *Texas Studies*, 13 (Summer 1971), 239–48, considers the possibility not only that Wordsworth's description of Snowdon may have influenced De Quincey's vision of Liverpool harbour but also that the influence may have been reciprocal, Wordsworth's revisions of the Snowdon passage profiting from a reading of De Quincey. For the most comprehensive and best documented study of the De Quincey-Wordsworth relation see John E. Jordan, *De Quincey to Wordsworth: A Biography of a Relationship With the Letters of Thomas De Quincey to the Wordsworth Family* (Berkeley: University of California Press 1962).
5 Cf a similar comment on this passage by Miller, *The Disappearance of God*, p 69.
6 The lines transcribed here (I have slightly truncated De Quincey's quotation) are from the *The Excursion*, II, 834–45.
7 *The Excursion*, II, 867–8, 873–4 (*The Poetical Works of William Wordsworth*, ed Thomas Hutchinson [London: Oxford University Press 1933]).
8 *Paradise Lost*, XII, 641–7 (*The Poetical Works of John Milton*, ed Helen Darbishire [Oxford: Clarendon Press, 1952], vol I).

NOTES TO CHAPTER 3

1 René Wellek, 'De Quincey's Status in the History of Ideas,' *Philological Quarterly*, 23 (July 1944), 269. Cf W.K. Wimsatt and Cleanth Brooks,

Literary Criticism: A Short History (New York: Knopf 1957), pp 426–7. Among the useful discussions of the theory of the literature of power are S.K. Proctor, *Thomas De Quincey's Theory of Literature* (Ann Arbor: University of Michigan Press 1943), pp 107–47; M.H. Abrams, *The Mirror and the Lamp: Romantic Theory and the Critical Tradition* (New York: Oxford University Press 1953), pp 143–4; and Clifford Leech, 'De Quincey as Literary Critic,' *Review of English Literature*, 2 (January 1961), 43–5.

2 Cf Wordsworth's characterization of the poet in the Preface to the Second Edition of *Lyrical Ballads* as a man of 'more than usual organic sensibility,' whose creations render the reader's 'affections strengthened and purified' (*Poetical Works*, II, 387–8); also Coleridge's reference to the poet, in Ch XIV of the *Biographia Literaria*, as one who 'brings the whole soul of man into activity' (*Biographia Literaria*, ed J. Shawcross [London: Oxford University Press 1907], II, 12).

3 For an interesting account of De Quincey's fascination with 'the triumphant power of the murderer' see Geoffrey Carnall, 'De Quincey on the Knocking at the Gate,' *Review of English Literature*, 2 (January 1961), 49–57.

4 Speaking of Poe, although what he says fits the context of 'The Knocking at the Gate' perfectly, Georges Poulet remarks that 'cut off from communication with the exterior world, the dream has its own interior place, circumscribed, independent of all other places. In a like manner ... the dream has its own time' (*Studies in Human Time*, trans Elliott Coleman [Baltimore: Johns Hopkins University Press 1956], p 330).

5 Mario Praz notes in this essay a 'humoristic evasion of a morbid obsession' (*The Romantic Agony*, trans Angus Davidson, 2nd ed [New York: Oxford University Press 1951], p 142).

6 See Lowery Nelson, 'Night Thoughts on the Gothic Novel,' *Yale Review*, 52 (Winter 1963), 236–57, for useful observations on this point.

7 See, e.g., his comic tales 'The King of Hayti' and 'The Incognito; or Count Fitz-Hum' (both adaptations from the German), in which the heroes assume disguises as death and as an omnipotent prince in order to gain the hand of an otherwise unattainable woman (see XII, 406–8, 431–2).

8 See H.A. Eaton, *Thomas De Quincey: A Biography* (New York: Oxford University Press 1936), pp 362–74.

9 Wolfgang Kayser, *The Grotesque in Art and Literature*, trans Ulrich Weisstein (Bloomington: Indiana University Press 1963) pp 185, 52.

10 Edward Sackville West, *A Flame in Sunlight: The Life and Work of Thomas De Quincey* (London: Cassell 1936), p 265.

11 For a full treatment of 'The Revolt of the Tartars' see my article 'Satanic Fall and Hebraic Exodus: An Interpretation of De Quincey's "Revolt of the Tartars",' *Studies in Romanticism*, 8 (Winter 1969), 95–108.

NOTES TO CHAPTER 4

1 See Sackville West, *A Flame in Sunlight*, pp 270–5.
2 H.A. Page (pseudonym of A.H. Japp), *Thomas De Quincey: His Life and Writings, with Unpublished Correspondence* (London: John Hogg 1877), I, 339.
3 For a more detailed account of the *Suspiria*'s complicated history of publication see Masson's introductory note to the series (XIII, 331–3) and Eaton, *Thomas De Quincey*, pp 427–8n.
4 This tendency to make autobiography mythic is most compactly seen in a kind of prospectus to the work as whole, attached as a note to 'Levana and Our Ladies of Sorrow.' In announcing the quadrapartite scheme of the *Suspiria*, each part devoted to a phase of personal experience, De Quincey assigns to these phases resonant titles such as 'The Pariah Worlds' and 'The Kingdom of Darkness,' as if they were regions of a visionary landscape (SP 246n).
5 Cf Ralph Haven Wolfe, 'Priest and Prophet: Thomas De Quincey and William Wordsworth in their Personal and Literary Relationship' (unpublished diss. Indiana 1961), pp 154–5.
6 Miller, *The Disappearance of God*, p 23.
7 Geoffrey Hartman, *Wordsworth's Poetry, 1787–1814* (New Haven: Yale University Press 1964), p 33.
8 The most useful account of this Neoplatonic 'epistrophe' or spiritual return, in its relation to Romanticism, appears in M.H. Abrams, *Natural Supernaturalism: Tradition and Revolution in Romantic Literature* (New York: Norton 1971), pp 148ff.
9 *Posthumous Works of Thomas De Quincey*, ed Alexander H. Japp (London: Heinemann 1891), I, 12.
10 Judson S. Lyon, *Thomas De Quincey* (New York: Twayne 1969), also sees two organizing clusters of concern in the *Suspiria*, one theoretical (pertaining to dreams) and one 'mythical' (centring on lost pariah figures) (pp 97–8). My own sense that the *Suspiria*'s underlying myth is concerned with personal imaginative strength is of course diammetrically opposed to Lyon's.
11 Blake is cited here and elsewhere in this chapter for illustrative reasons. One senses the presence of the universal man in these visions not through some adventitious comparison with Blake (of whom De Quincey knew probably only a little) but rather in the likely influence of the ancient mystical tradition of the macrocosmic man, the cabbalic 'Adam Kadmon,' which both Blake and De Quincey, among other Romantics, put to use in their imagery. See Abrams, *Natural Supernaturalism*, pp 158 ff, for a useful discussion of this tradition of the cosmic man.

12 A curious analogue to this process occurs in some speculations of Marx, which try to account for the charm that ancient literature retains in an industrial age. Marx associates the 'childhood' of civilization with individual childhood and suggests that one's nostalgia for the latter extends itself to the former. See Peter Demetz, *Marx, Engels, and the Poets*, trans Jeffrey L. Sammons (Chicago: University of Chicago Press 1967), pp 68–9.

13 The notion of the Dark Interpreter as a 'second self' appears in Cooper, *The Prose Poetry of Thomas De Quincey*, pp 45–6; Moreux sees in the Dark Interpreter the archetypal figure of the underworld guide (*Thomas De Quincey*, p 491), whereas Porter views the figure as a 'mediator between the destructive and redemptive powers in De Quincey' ('The Double Self,' p 144).

14 Northrop Frye notes the resemblance of Savannah-la-Mar to Atlantis in 'The Drunken Boat,' *Romanticism Reconsidered*, ed Northrop Frye (New York: Columbia University Press 1963), p 18.

15 Cf. the analogous (but more macabre) city in the sea of Poe, which Georges Poulet considers as a metaphor for the dream world (*Studies in Human Time*, p 330).

16 See Miller, *The Disappearance of God*, p 73.

17 See *Posthumous Works*, I, 16–23.

NOTES TO CHAPTER 5

1 Ernst Theodor Sehrt, *Religiöses und geschichtliches Denken bei T. De Quincey (1785–1859)* (Berlin: Junker und Dünnhaupt 1936), p 37. A more recent treatment of De Quincey's views on these subjects, particularly relevant to his conservative attitudes on war, appears in Robert Hopkins, 'De Quincey on War and the Pastoral Design of *The English Mail-Coach*,' *Studies in Romanticism*, 6 (Spring 1967), 129–51.

2 *Posthumous Works*, I, 166. The line of verse quoted by De Quincey in this passage is from Wordsworth's sonnet 'Advance – come forth from thy Tyrolean ground' (1809).

3 *Thomas De Quincey: His Life and Writings*, I, 325.

4 Ibid, p 340.

5 See Frederick Burwick, 'The Dream-Visions of Jean Paul and Thomas De Quincey,' *Comparative Literature*, 20 (Winter 1968), 1–26, for a study of Jean Paul's influence on De Quincey's dream-visions; see in particular pp 16–19 for a detailed comparison of the 'Traum über das All' and the 'Dream-Vision of the Infinite.'

6 Commentators on De Quincey's acknowledged master in this work, Jean Paul, have made observations that are in fact more particularly applicable

to De Quincey here than to Jean Paul's 'Traum.' Kayser remarks that Jean Paul seems filled not only with fear that 'the heavenly gates will never open, but also with doubt whether they really are the heavenly gates at all. The poet of seraphic ... moods felt constantly urged to create abysmal visions, those nightmares of destruction and terror inspired by the knowledge that there is no God' (*The Grotesque in Art and Literature*, p 56). In *Jean Paul's Dreams* (London: Oxford University Press 1966) J.W. Smeed comments on the German writer's fear of 'an afterlife in which the only God is a foul personification of destruction and decay; it derives not from the believer's fear of damnation, but from the despair and cheated hope of the sceptic' (p 32).

7 Hopkins, 'De Quincey on War,' p 136. A number of points in this most useful commentary parallel my own, although our general emphases differ; in particular, I tend to find far more ironic qualification of the Christian affirmation in which the *Mail-Coach* ostensibly concludes.

8 A thorough geneaology of the apocalyptic image of the chariot, with a fuller discussion of the indissoluble unity of its components, appears in Harold Bloom, *Shelley's Mythmaking* (New Haven: Yale University Press 1959), pp 231–6. See also Northrop Frye, *Fearful Symmetry: A Study of William Blake* (Princeton: Princeton University Press 1947), pp 272–4. For a detailed study of this descent of the image, from the myth of the charioteer in the *Phaedrus* and the story of Elijah in 2 Kings, with appropriate comments on *The English Mail-Coach*, see Sander L. Gilman, 'The Uncontrollable Steed: A Study of the Metamorphosis of a Literary Image,' *Euphorion*, 6 (1972), 32–54.

9 Northrop Frye, in a context relating to Shelley, alludes to 'De Quincey's powerful essay,' observing in the symbol of the mail-coach 'a new kind of personality which is at once human and mechanical. As that it is partly demonic, a Juggernaut with a baleful dragon eye, bearing news of victory and death' (*A Study of English Romanticism* [New York: Random House 1968], p 93). De Quincey, who late in the *Mail-Coach* associates the vehicle with 'Death the crowned phantom,' may well have been influenced by the famous ch XX of *Dombey and Son* (1847–8), a work he is known to have read (see XIII, 206 for an allusion); for Dickens the vehicular form of destruction is the railway: 'The power that forced itself upon its iron way ... defiant of all paths and roads, piercing through the heart of every obstacle, ... was a type of the triumphant monster, Death' (*Dombey and Son*, New Oxford Illustrated Dickens [London: Oxford University Press 1950], p 280). Frederick S. Rockwell, 'De Quincey and the Ending of *Moby Dick*,' *Nineteenth-Century Fiction*, 9 (December 1954), 161–8, presents a plausible argument for the influence of *The English Mail-Coach* on Melville.

10 Hopkins, 'De Quincey on War,' p 145.

11 Cf Hopkins (p 146), who makes essentially the same point and suggests the influence of Carlyle's *Past and Present*, in its discussions of modern industrial labour, upon this portion of the *Mail-Coach*.

12 The whole episode, graphically considered, is almost embarrassingly phallic: powerful and uncontrollable animal forces plunging down a straight and tunnel-like path towards a fragile and feminine beauty.

13 Cf an unassimilated fragment of the *Suspiria* left by De Quincey in manuscript: 'Mystery unfathomable of Death! Mystery unapproachable of God! Destined it was, from the foundations of the world, that each mystery should make war upon the other: once that the lesser mystery should swallow up for a moment a *limbus* of the greater; and that woe is past; once that the greater mystery should swallow for ever the whole vortex of the lesser; and that glory is yet to come' (*Posthumous Works*, I, 24).

14 Cf a posthumously published fragment on the principle of evil: 'Not only must the energies of destruction be equal to those of creation, but in fact, perhaps by trespassing a little of the first upon the last, is the true advance sustained; for it must be an advance as well as a balance. But you say this will but in other words mean that forces devoted (and properly so) to production and creation are absorbed by destruction. True; but the opposing phenomenon will be going on in a large ratio, and each must react on the other. The productive must meet and correspond to the destructive. The destructive must revise and stimulate the continued production' (*Posthumous Works*, I, 172). This is virtually a restatement of Blake's myth of the Prolific and the Devourer in *The Marriage of Heaven and Hell*, without any of Blake's subversive ironies or ethical revaluations. Advance and balance, the two co-ordinates of contrapuntal music, appear as ends in themselves.

15 Cf Miller, *The Disappearance of God*, who, noting the pattern of descent into darkness and sudden ascent into light, derives from this and other passages in De Quincey's writings (notably from the essay 'On the Supposed Scriptural Expression for Eternity,' to be found in *De Quincey and his Friends*, ed James Hogg [London 1895], pp 295–313) the concept that evil must come into being and hold sway in the world so that it may inevitably die: 'So much suffering is [man's] allotted fate in "the secret proportions of a heavenly scale." Only when he has exhausted that measure of pain which is his own *aeon* as a creature of mixed evil and good can he escape the wheel of suffering, consign his evil to eternal oblivion, and enter, by right of his anchorage in the divine good, into eternal participation in God's *aeon*' (pp 75–6). Miller does not go on,

however, to inquire into the *raison d'être* of so arbitrary a scheme. The fact that the scheme *is* arbitrary is its most important characteristic; it fulfils an imaginative craving for the symmetries of a totally apprehended pattern.

16 For a careful analysis of De Quincey's organization of recurrent phrases and episodic motifs so as to imitate the traditional fugal structure see Calvin S. Brown, Jr, 'The Musical Structure of De Quincey's *Dream-Fugue*,' *The Musical Quarterly*, 24 (July 1938), 341–50.

NOTES TO CHAPTER 6

1 The 'Postscript' to 'Murder' retains some of the Gothic elements of De Quincey's earlier writings, such as an 'all-conquering' murderer (XIII, 89) and a Janus-vision of demonic and ordinary worlds meeting at a threshold – in the form of the murderer and a servant girl poised in tense anticipation on opposite sides of a closed door (XIII, 86–9). But these elements are located firmly in a Dickensian world of ordinary shopkeepers, engagingly described (XIII, 81–2), and the scenes of murder are described with laconic detachment and the painstaking detail of a first-rate reporter.

2 It may seem unreasonable to posit the existence of any such 'imagination of 1853' when the evidence for it derives from a concatenation of pieces published at scattered intervals in a period of nearly twenty years and written under different moods and for different journals. But the anachronism of viewing the *Sketches* as a corporate entity is more apparent than real; De Quincey was both fastidious and assiduous in his revisions and rearrangements, as his treatment of the *Suspiria* material shows. Additions and revisions stud the quarried material, and enormous sections of the latter part of the sketches (e.g., I, 332–416) were written in 1853 and yet maintain the characteristic mood of the *Tait* material which they follow. One may speak properly of an editorial imagination whose products are as worthy of critical study as those of an original creative impulse. See Elizabeth W. Bruss, *Autobiographical Acts: The Changing Situation of a Literary Genre* (Baltimore: Johns Hopkins University Press 1976), pp 96–101, for a treatment of *Autobiographic Sketches* as a coherent work; Bruss provides (pp 101–26) a sustained and subtle comparison of the *Sketches* and *Suspiria de Profundis* as alternative versions of autobiography.

3 See, e.g., Moreux, *Thomas de Quincey*, pp 474–5; Sackville West, *A Flame in Sunlight*, pp 300–1; and Ian Jack, 'De Quincey Revises His *Confessions*' PMLA, 72 (March 1957), 145–6. Jack's essay remains the best detailed study of the differences between the two versions.

4 Page, *Thomas De Quincey*, II, 111.

5 Both of these works take their protagonists from a bondage closely connected to Christian institutions into a punishing wilderness, the Asiatic
steppes for the Tartars, the heights of the Andes for the Spanish Nun, a
wilderness which provides both an arena of crisis and access to rewarding
pastoral landscapes. It seems that De Quincey has had to establish these
themes in exotic disguises before he can finally bring them home, as it
were, to inform his own personal exerience. A jocular reference to the
Nun's memoirs as 'The Confessions of a Biscayan Fire-Eater' (XIII, 241)
suggests his conscious awareness of the similarity between the pattern of
her history and that of his own.

6 'Such words as "echo," "repeat," "magnify," "amplify," "swell," "revive,"
"agitate," "duplicate," and "reverberate" are more than fortuitously
numerous throughout the text,' notes Kathleen Blake in 'The Whispering
Gallery and Structural Coherence in De Quincey's Revised *Confessions of
an English Opium-Eater*,' *Studies in English Literature*, 13 (Autumn 1973),
640. This is an excellent study of the Gallery image.

7 Cf Porter on this point: 'De Quincey's world is one of contingencies, both
of real events which threaten his peace and ambitions, and of preter-
natural, symbolic forces which the imagination creates only to turn back
upon the self. He is finally a victim not so much of the "dark oracular
legislation external to myself" but of the self which creates this menacing
world' ('The Double Self,' p 112).

8 Hayter suggests a direct influence of Wordsworth's passage upon De
Quincey's depiction of the Bore (*Opium and the Romantic Imagination*,
p 243). The dream of the flood became De Quincey's favourite passage in
The Prelude and he quotes from it extensively in his biographical essay on
Wordsworth (see II, 268–70).

9 Several of De Quincey's critics have questioned the biographical authen-
ticity of some episodes in the *Confessions*. Moreux cites the dream-like
way in which many of the incidents unfold and speaks generally of 'une
cueieuse atmosphère d'irréalité' (*Thomas De Quincey*, p 472). More specifically, Sackville West conjectures plausibly about the possible inauthen-
ticity of the story of 'Monsieur Monsieur De Quincey' (*A Flame in
Sunlight*, p 50).

10 Cf similar comments in Miller, *The Disappearance of God*, p 34.

NOTES TO CHAPTER 7

1 Frank Kermode, *The Sense of an Ending: Studies in the Theory of Fiction*
(New York: Oxford University Press 1967), p 173.

2 See Jorge Luis Borges, 'The Mirror of Enigmas,' trans James E. Irby, in *Labyrinths: Selected Stories and Other Writings*, ed Donald A. Yates and James E. Irby (New York: New Directions 1964), p 209.
3 'Ode: Intimations of Immortality,' lines 144–5; *The Prelude*, VI, 608; 'Tintern Abbey,' lines 50, 56.

ঞ Index ঞ

taneity of past time in 70, 72–3,
79–81; the dream-state 43, 59–60,
70, 94–6, 106, 107, 154; imagination, ambivalence towards 144,
146, 147–9; imagination, autonomy
of 21–4, 39, 47, 56, 65, 66–70
passim, 81, 140, 144, 147; imagination, as developing from personal
loss 7, 21, 30, 60, 63, 71–2, 115,
130–1; individual life as archetypal
form 6–7, 58, 61, 74–81 *passim*, 155,
156; and opium 12, 20–2, 33, 57, 59,
69, 124, 145, 153; Romantic myth-
making 3, 9, 58, 148–9
– and the self: as alienated and
impotent 5–6, 19–20, 24–6, 32, 49,
54–5, 89, 96, 118–19, 128, 138–40;
anxiety and dread 5, 25, 29–30, 44,
46, 49, 50, 89, 94, 96, 99, 102–3, 116,
123, 128, 130, 132–4, 140–1; assertiveness and self-liberation 56, 123,
128, 129–31, 132–6 *passim*, 137,
141–2, 144–5, 149–50; innocence, as
communal experience 16–19, 55,
61–2; loss and bereavement 5, 7, 8,
62–8 *passim*, 71, 143–4 (*see also* as
visionary: imagination, as developing from personal loss; recurring
images and motifs in works of:
female figures, dying or lost);
repose, quest for 6, 56, 128–9, 130,
137, 143, 144; sexuality 100, 102–3,
107, 157; solitude and isolation
20–1, 60–1, 68
– theological themes in: death as harmonious process 5–6, 8, 30, 62, 64,
78–9; Death, personified 5, 93–4,
105, 107, 157; the demonic 29–30,
42–3, 47–8, 101–2, 141; deviations
from Christian orthodoxy 72, 86,
96, 114, 157; the Fall of man 33–4,

55, 106, 107, 114, 125, 146; God 23,
65, 79–81, 86–8, 92, 95–6, 110,
114–15; God and death, relation
of 66, 84, 90, 96, 114, 116, 157;
mysticism 22–3, 65–6, 155
– on power: allegiance to order and
authority 87–8, 100, 103, 106, 124,
133, 136; British nationalism and
imperialism 85, 87, 99–114 *passim*;
murder 41–2, 44–7, 159; the Napoleonic Wars 87, 98, 104, 110–14
passim; power as imaginative concept 8, 36–9, 40–56 *passim*, 97–8,
140, 144, 148; progress, historical
and technological 84–8, 92–3, 96,
98, 105; tyrannical government 49,
50–1, 88; violence as a mode of
power 5, 39–47 *passim*, 88, 94,
99–115 *passim*, 128
– concepts of symbolism in: correspondences between the finite and
the transcendent 10–11, 38, 59–60,
148–9; 'involutes' as symbols 63–4,
67, 78–9, 92, 124; projection or
externalizing of psychological
states 12, 15, 20, 23, 38, 50, 68, 94,
103, 106, 123, 128–9, 140–1
– as prose writer: digression in prose
of 10, 120, 152; displacement
modes in prose of 10, 13, 20, 34, 35,
44–6, 48, 134–5, 146; 'impassioned
prose' 8–9, 58, 148, 152; miscella-
neous style and subject matter in
prose of 9–11, 54–5, 96–7, 120;
realism and demythologizing in
prose of 9–10, 117–21, 146, 159
– genres in prose of: autobiography
7, 35, 59, 69–70, 81–3, 118–21, 122,
150, 151; fiction 35, 47, 52; the
Gothic 5, 47, 48–53 *passim*, 159; the
grotesque 52–3; the 'literature of

This book
was designed by
WILLIAM RUETER
and was printed by
University of
Toronto
Press